BOOKS BY RICHARD A. WATSON

Nonfiction

The Downfall of Cartesianism

Man and Nature: An Anthropological Essay in Human Ecology with Patty Jo Watson

The Longest Cave with Roger W. Brucker

The Philosopher's Diet: How to Lose Weight and Change the World

The Breakdown of Cartesian Metaphysics

The Philosopher's Joke: Essays in Form and Content

Fiction

The Runner

Under Plowman's Floor

Writing Philosophy

A Guide to Professional Writing and Publishing

Richard A. Watson

Southern Illinois University Press
Carbondale and Edwardsville

Copyright © 1992 by the Board of Trustees,
Southern Illinois University

Printed in the United States of America

Designed by Kyle Lake

Production supervised by Natalia Nadraga

95 94 93 92   4 3 2 1

Library of Congress Cataloging-in-Publication Data

Watson, Richard A., 1931–
    Writing philosophy: a guide to professional writing and
publishing / Richard A. Watson.
        p.   cm.
    Includes bibliographical references.
    1. Philosophy—Authorship.   I. Title.
B52.7.W37   1992
808'.0661—dc20   91-32298
ISBN 0-8093-1810-5   CIP

The paper used in this publication meets the minimum requirements of
American National Standard for Information Sciences—Permanence of
Paper for Printed Library Materials, ANSI Z39.48-1984. ∞

Cum grano salis
—old philosopher's recipe

CONTENTS

PREFACE

Philosophical writing is a technical skill that must be learned if a philosopher is to spread his or her ideas further than among a circle of immediate acquaintances. More than that, despite the importance of the oral tradition in philosophy and the influence of the dialogue, many philosophical points and positions are so intricate and complex that they can be advanced, followed, and criticized only if they are printed as stepwise arguments for study and contemplation at length and at leisure. In this guide I provide a set of basic principles and a plan for writing argumentative papers of 1,050 to 10,500 words (3 to 30 printed pages) in length and books containing a sequence of sustained arguments of 70,000 to 105,000 words (200 to 300 printed pages).*

The first book of most professional philosophers will be a rewritten Ph.D. dissertation. Consequently, I provide a plan for writing a dissertation in such a way that its chapters can do double duty as articles and the dissertation as a whole can be published with very little revision as a book. Other than the practicality of this plan in terms of economy and prudence, I offer in its favor the observation that if at least one article derived from a dissertation is not publishable, serious questions arise as to whether it was worth writing and whether its author is qualified as a professional philosopher.

This said, a young assistant professor read the manuscript of this book with increasing depression and anger. She did

*This guide can be used by anyone who is faced with the task of writing a paper, thesis, or book in which arguments must be given for conclusions. The principles are general and the commentaries have wide scope. Thus, they can easily be applied to work in all areas of the social sciences and humanities.

not deny that it contains excellent advice for getting ahead in academe, but she deplored the approach. Philosophy, she said, should be done out of love of knowledge. Philosophy is not a business. Bright young philosophers should not be told to get ideas by scanning the journals but should be encouraged to work on the ideas that already excite them. Of course, they must be instructed in the basics, but after that the discipline of writing philosophy should be undertaken not just to turn out a publishable product but to do the hard work of thinking things out.

I agree that the ultimate and primary goal is to be a good philosopher. So why have I written a guide recommending that you write your first papers and book the way some people eat cold cuts on a plate? Because no matter how deep is their love of knowledge, most philosophers in America have to support themselves by teaching in colleges and universities. And whatever anyone says to the contrary, the criterion used overwhelmingly to determine whether or not you get tenure is professional publication. Publishing alone is not even enough. Your work also has to be good. But you do have to publish. Soon. Six years after you finish your Ph.D., the reckoning will be in. The time is long past when administrators could be convinced to give tenure to someone merely because that person exhibits great promise or even genius.

I was further encouraged by the fact that during its composition, several versions of this guide were very well received by graduate students and untenured faculty members in several departments at several universities. My young colleague who objected so strenuously left college teaching because she did not want to do the writing and publishing required to earn tenure. (As we go to press, she has returned to academe and will do well.)

But what about teaching? That's another book. I hope you are and want to be an excellent teacher, but in almost all four-year colleges and universities in America, good teaching alone is not enough. If you don't publish, you won't get tenure, whatever the regulations and the administrators say.

This is not a guide for getting tenure. It is a guide to

professional writing and publishing, which, as I stress above, are essential if you are to enter the community of scholars and participate in the conversation and discussions that constitute philosophy. But also, to the extent that publication is the crucial factor in most tenure decisions, it will help you meet tenure criteria.

I refuse to be embarrassed about writing a guide that will help young scholars both to write systematically and to get tenure. And it would be wrong of them to be intimidated by snobbish colleagues who tell them that it is beneath a scholar's dignity to worry about job security. That conceit is an affectation deriving from a time when only second sons of rich noble families became professors or Oxford dons. But today very few scholars have independent incomes. Thus, it is insensitive and anachronistic to scorn concern with and anguish over what is *the* crucial practical problem in the lives of young scholars today. They must get tenure to have careers in academe. After lawyers and medical doctors get their degrees, they must pass state board examinations to secure their careers. Young scholars must get tenure. Thus, no one in academe should pretend that we are above such mundane concerns as recognizing and preparing for the tenure examination. It is romantic nonsense to deplore or ignore the fact that competition for places in the ivory tower is as tough as anywhere else.

No, the tenure system is not the world's best. (But see J. H. Hexter's "Publish or Perish: A Defense.") I might have written a utopian tract about the ideal university, but I don't have any practical ideas about how to change the system. I don't even believe that the method of determining scholarly merit by publication is bad, although its application to tenure decisions is sometimes too rigid. So I have written this guide for those who *do* love knowledge, for those who can be very good philosophers, for those who can enrich their own lives and the lives of others in academe. What I describe herein is not just an intellectual game: it is a professional skill essential to being a good philosopher and a member of the wider philosophical community. But to the extent that it is like a game, you must play it well to earn your right to be a professional philosopher in this business society. It is better than being chosen because of your race, religion, class, family, age, sex, good looks, or charming personality. And even in America, you can't ordinarily buy tenure, only an honorary degree.

I want to take this opportunity to thank four philosophers who separately taught me some of these things: Robert G. Turnbull, Gustav Bergmann, William K. Frankena, and Richard H. Popkin. I learned from them collectively that of all the requirements for writing philosophy, none is more critical than a delicate sensitivity to nuance combined with an ability to come right out and say what you mean.

I have profited from comments by (and now I thank) the following people, who have read this work in manuscript: Dorothy Fleck, John Fodor, Dan Gunter, Charles F. Hildebolt, Rebecca Holsen (who provided the Orwell quotation and the anecdote about Sidney Morgenbesser), Jack W. Meiland, Steven S. Schwarzschild, Teddy Seidenfeld, Alfred J. Stenner, Constance Urdang, Patty Jo Watson, Rubie Watson, Alison Wylie, Joyce Trebilcot, two anonymous referees who had extensive influence, and Carl P. Wellman, who takes the prize for making me delete an entire page about a compelling—but apparently bogus—contrast between 'compare with' and 'compare to'.

I thank also the editors of *Theoria* and the *History of Philosophy Quarterly* for permission to reprint material that appeared in their journals.

Finally, I thank Philip E. Converse, Director, and Robert A. Scott, Associate Director, and all the rest of the fine staff at the Center for Advanced Study in the Behavioral Sciences, Stanford, California, where so much of my philosophical writing has been done and where the final revision and preparation of the manuscript for publication was completed. I am grateful for financial support provided by The Andrew W. Mellon Foundation.

1

INTRODUCTION

If you want to be a professional philosopher, you must publish. This is because publishing is almost the only way you can enter the dialogue—the conversation—that is the lifeblood of philosophy. In discussion notes, articles, and books you present your theses, arguments, and criticisms to your peers. Their response is the test and measure of your philosophizing. The interchange constitutes philosophy, and your participation in it will help make you a good philosopher.

The traditional form of philosophical discussion is argument—the presentation of cogent and logically connected evidence and reasons for some conclusion. In the dialogues of Plato, Berkeley, and Hume; in medieval disputations and the *Summa* of Saint Thomas Aquinas; in the *Meditations, Objections, and Replies* of Descartes; in the volumes of Schilpp's Library of Living Philosophers; and in the most recent philosophical journals, overwhelmingly you will find arguments for and against stated positions.

In fact, not all philosophical writing is argumentative. Augustine is confessional, Thomas à Kempis is edifying, Rousseau is persuasive, Hegel is speculative, Nietzsche is bombastic, Kierkegaard pleads, Fichte exhorts, and J. L. Austin provides therapy. Nor have all well-known philosophers published. Socrates and Pyrrho did not publish at all: but neither did they teach in a university. Wittgenstein published very little: but he wrote a lot and his manuscripts were avidly circulated and were very influential, a most elegant and confirmatory sort of publication and response.

Nor is the argumentative style always the most felicitous.

1

The writings of one of the greatest argumentative philosophers, G. E. Moore, can be downright boring. And some philosophers of genius, such as Heidegger, convince in texts where argument is overwhelmed or absent. Sometimes even great arguers such as William James and Bertrand Russell write so excellently with such distinctive styles that they persuade despite faulty arguments.

Original philosophers and writers of genius sometimes can dispense with argument, but most professional philosophers cannot. Argument remains the core of most philosophizing. Argument has sustained many a noble career in philosophy. Budding professional philosophers must begin with argumentative writing, and many of them will not (need not, and probably should not) go beyond it. I have written this guide for them.

2

PRINCIPLES

A. REASON

Philosophy is distinguished from theology, politics, and poetics by its dependence on reason as the ultimate criterion of evaluation. Reason demands internal consistency, and so the basic principle of philosophy is the principle of noncontradiction: a thing cannot be both *A* and *not A* in the same way at the same time, or, in propositional terms, a philosophical system cannot contain both the proposition *p* and the proposition *not p*. In all of philosophy, the flaw that always rules a position or argument out of play is lack of logical consistency. No appeal to authority, faith, beauty, bedazzlement, interest, morality, emotion, or force can override an internal contradiction. Thus, the first rule in philosophical writing is *Be consistent*.

B. CLARITY

Philosophical writing is similar to scientific writing in the requirement that it be clear. This requirement follows in part from the demand for consistency, which is monitored primarily by avoidance of ambiguous words and expressions. In the name of clarity, plain writing is preferred to rhetorical flourishes. This requirement means that one must say what one means as nearly as possible with univocal words and phrases, in detail, and at sufficient length to avoid misunderstanding. This seldom results in beautiful or evocative writing, but when practiced by a master such as Moore, philosophical writing exhibits the elegance of precision. Clarity does not necessarily rule out ambiguity, but ambiguities must be clearly evident and not hidden. This demand for clarity, like that for consistency, is in itself almost a definition of philosophy as an attempt to understand and to be understood fully and without confusion. On this definition of philosophy based on reason, geniuses who write unclearly may persuade, but if their positions are not reducible to clear exposition, they eventually are classified as poets, prophets, or mystics, not as philosophers.

C. ARGUMENT

It is not enough for a philosophical paper to be consistent and clear; it must also have a point that is supported by an argument. Inspirational and edifying discourses have points, but they can be persuasive even if they are inconsistent and unclear. In philosophical writing, the point one wishes to make can be established only by presenting it as the conclusion of an argument. Sometimes the point of a philosophical book itself is spoken of as an argument, as in, "The argument of this book is that philosophical positions can be supported only by appeal to reason." Arguments within a philosophical presentation are sequential logical developments of premises, statements of evidence, and inferences resulting in the position or statement that is the point of the presentation.

3

WRITING A PHILOSOPHICAL PAPER

A. HOW TO BEGIN

A philosophical paper must bear on a philosophical problem. You can set out to expostulate, interpret, clarify, analyze, explicate, develop, reduce, derive, dissolve, solve, or give the history of a philosophical problem, but in each case the problem itself is primary. The problem and how you approach it should be indicated in the title and fully identified in the first paragraph. Here is a model sentence for beginning a standard philosophical paper: "In the following, I argue that a philosophical paper must have a philosophical problem as its heart." A beginning sentence of this sort should be followed by a short step-by-step statement of the argument that supports the conclusion and that will be developed in the paper. Thus, philosophy papers are written the way murder mysteries often are, with the conclusion known in advance; but unlike mystery writers, philosophers strive throughout to make the reader follow an open and correct line of reasoning to the conclusion.

You must, of course, have a problem to work on. Some people apparently cannot recognize philosophical problems. That is why among formulae of praise in letters of recommendation written by philosophy professors one often finds the line, "This person knows what a philosophical problem is." Most introductions to philosophy are designed to exhibit philosophical problems to students in the hope that they will catch on. Students who not only understand but also can advance discussion about philosophical problems are said to have philosophical aptitude. A book designed to exhibit philosophical problems and to lead readers to specific solutions is Bertrand Russell's *Problems of Philosophy*. I assume that you know what a philosophical problem is. The problem is to find one to work on.

Most beginners make one of two major mistakes: they tackle either too large a problem or several problems at once. You cannot adequately cover the problem of other minds from Plato to Descartes in a dissertation, let alone in a thirty-page paper. You might be able to handle Leibniz on other minds in a three-hundred-page dissertation, and a single version of an argument for other minds in a thirty-page paper. Even here, there is an enormous literature on other minds, on Leibniz, and on Leibniz on other minds. Thus, if you begin with a problem chosen from the general literature, you may be overwhelmed by lack of knowledge as to which sources and which secondary literature to read. Consequently, I recommend that beginners start on very small, exactly specified problems. Such problems are ideal projects for term papers.

To find a manageable, small philosophical problem to work on for your first paper, go to the library and look in recent philosophical journals for papers on topics that interest you. Read a dozen or so of these articles (this will give you some notion of how philosophical papers are written and how philosophical problems are treated) until you have a philosophical idea while reading one of them. This idea at this stage of your career is most likely to be a way either of criticizing or of developing a point made in a published article.

Now read all the references cited in that article. This may be enough, but you might want to pursue some of the references in the references. You should also look around for other recent articles on the same topic. But don't search too far. The article you are criticizing contains a specific problem, and you have isolated one feature of that problem. One virtue of this procedure is that the form of your paper is preset. You are restricted to criticizing one explicit point. In other words, the easiest first paper for you to write is a note or a comment as a contribution to an ongoing discussion. Philosophers working in the area have already set the boundaries for you, and as long as you stick to the small point you want to make, you can make a contribution that is as solid as any the most experienced philosophers could make. More than one beginning philosopher has made his reputation by pointing out a serious error in an important philosopher's work.

Your manuscript might not be longer than half a dozen pages. This exercise is thus calculated to teach you a very important skill in philosophical writing, which is that of sticking to one point. A note or comment should be confined to a single point, and publishing restrictions demand that what you have to say be said in as few words as possible. You should rewrite this first paper until it is nothing but a specialized instrument bearing exactly and only on the point you are making. If you start with a seven-page manuscript, you might in the end reduce it to a three-page manuscript.

This procedure is the easiest way to find and define a problem, but it nevertheless presents you with a hard writing assignment. You are restricted to one point, which makes it easy, but you *must* have a viable point, because if you don't, the paring down of your text and the concision that is demanded in such a short manuscript will expose ruthlessly any inadequacies in your argument. It is a very good test of your ability to detect a philosophical problem (to show that you know what one is) and of your philosophical aptitude (to show that you can make a philosophical move from one point to another). For examples, go to the journals and begin reading articles, notes, and comments.

B. HOW TO WRITE AN ARTICLE

After you have written several notes and comments, you should be able to make a single point. Now you can write an article in which you make one point supported by one extensive argument or by several short arguments. There are numerous exceptions to the following plan, but a good way to begin is with this formal outline:

1. Introduction

A beginning paragraph about half a page long and never more than one page long that begins with the phrase "In this paper I show," followed by the conclusion or point you want to make. The second sentence goes: "My arguments for this conclusion are (1) . . . , (2) . . . , (3) . . . ."

2. Body of the Paper

One-page introduction to the problem, followed by several sections, each of which presents part of an extensive argument or one of several short arguments for the conclusion. Each of these sections can be constructed on the model of the short discussion pieces you have been writing.

3. Conclusion

Three pages, beginning with the sentences: "In this paper I have shown. . . . My arguments for this conclusion are (1) . . . , (2) . . . , (3) . . . ." This is *not* a repetition of your introduction but is rather a concise summary of your paper for a reader who can now understand a short, dense presentation because you have made your general argument clear in the body of the paper. The conclusion can also contain a general or specific point that derives from but extends beyond the presentation in the three main sections of the paper.

4. Abstract

Abstracts are from one hundred to three hundred words long. Compose your abstract by summarizing the combined texts of your introduction and conclusion. If you cannot do this—if all the important points in your paper are not included in the introduction and conclusion—then they are inadequate.

A colleague responded to this outline in outrage as follows: "These cut-and-dried rules would have killed off most good writers of philosophy at the start. Does Whitehead write this way? Russell? Nietzsche?" My answer is that Nietzsche never wrote this way, Whitehead did in his most accessible work, and Russell almost always did but was so good a writer that you seldom notice. *Really good* writers always go their own way. This is a guide for beginning philosophers who aspire to be professionals. It will not harm anyone who is already a good writer, nor will it smother genius.

Should you outline the paper in detail, as you were taught to do in high school? Perhaps. Making such an outline will require you to think precisely what your point is, about the arguments that support it, and how your thesis can best be presented. Some people make elaborate outlines, several pages long, and then when they sit down to write they have merely to fill in the spaces.

Another way to proceed is to sit down and write out freely what you have to say. The writing itself is a thinking process in which you can try out arguments and ideas. When you get everything down on paper, then you can look at it, reorganize it, and rewrite it. In effect, this approach is to outline the paper after you have written the first draft.

If you outline your paper thoroughly before writing it, don't get trapped. Philosophy, after all, is the art of getting out of boxes. If you see something wrong with your original plan while writing or see a better way to present a point, then deviate from your outline. This may seem to be unnecessary advice, but philosophers often fall in love with neat structures. Should form ever override content? In logic, sure; but what is the relation of form to content in ordinary sentences? That's a tough one.

However (you see how the predetermined form of this discussion carries us along comfortably), the danger with writing it all out before making an outline or plan is that you may become so attached to the first version of your paper that you resist rewriting it. William Faulkner said, "Strangle your babies," by which he meant that you must overcome the inclination to preserve and protect your first draft. You must scrutinize it very carefully to eliminate repetitions and irrelevancies, to get the order of your arguments right, and to make sure your words say what you mean.

It is probably best to make an initial outline, no matter how rudimentary. Then write down what you have to say, and on the basis of this draft, improve the outline. Do you have to write out the outline? No, just keep it in mind, for your paper will have some sort of structure even if you don't plan it; it is best if you impose the order in your paper yourself so you have control of what is going on.

Your first article probably will be a development of one of your discussion notes. A discussion note might itself be used as one of the main sections of the paper. I recommend that you try to revise and develop your writing in this cumulative way. After you have written several articles, one of them can be revised as a chapter of your dissertation, perhaps the introductory chapter. And of course you should choose your dissertation topic with an eye to turning the dissertation into a book manuscript.

This is a general plan. I cannot actually tell you how to write a paper in this short book. Or, rather, if I did I would be mostly duplicating what has already been written about writing an argumentative paper in four excellent books: *Philosophical Writing* by A. P. Martinich, *College Thinking* by Jack W. Meiland, *The Practice of Philosophy* by Jay Rosenberg, and *A Rulebook for Arguments* by Anthony Weston. I recommend that you read these books, but the best way to learn to write is to find a professor who both knows how to write an argumentative paper and is willing to read and discuss your papers critically. I believe that writing is so important to philosophers that all philosophy professors should teach students how to write, but not all professors agree with me. Find a professor who will criticize your papers and make you rewrite them over and over again until your argument is clear.

C. WHERE TO PUBLISH

Notes, comments, and articles should always be written for a specific journal. A note or comment on a given article should be sent to the journal in which that article appeared.

Type your manuscript in the form specified by that journal. Some journals do not accept notes and comments, so then you must go to journals such as *Mind* that regularly publish discussion notes.

If your ambition is to publish, say, in the *American Philosophical Quarterly*, then you should read all the issues of that journal for the last three years cover to cover. This gives you a general sense of the problems the editor is interested in, and it also gives you a feeling for "the *APQ* article." It will do you no good at all to send a *Journal of the History of Philosophy* article even to the *Journal of the History of Ideas*. Editors are quite sensitive to genre differences, and you must attain this sensitivity, too, if you want to publish.

This concern with form and type is not merely a matter of school, editorial bias, or traditional idiosyncrasy. Philosophy is practiced in many different modes, and the sometimes subtle differences in vocabulary, syntax, style, subject, and method indicate real and often important philosophical differences. You can learn about philosophy by taking the standard courses and by reading the classic works, including some by contemporary giants such as Willard Van Orman Quine. But you cannot learn how philosophy is being done—how to do philosophy—in your own time unless you follow the many arguments and discussions in the journals. The subtle differences between journal-article genres do reflect serious philosophical differences. You must know them to keep from mixing genres in your own papers. What might seem to you to be a perfectly reasonable set of arguments may not be publishable because it combines two different forms of presentation, argument, methodological style, or even (or especially) syntax and vocabulary.

Besides reading the journals themselves, you should look in the *Guidebook for Publishing Philosophy* prepared by Marcia Yudkin and Janice M. Moulton for the American Philosophical Association. It contains information about how to prepare and submit manuscripts, plus detailed specifications about most of the North American philosophy journals and publishers.

Send your manuscript addressed to the editor by name,

for example, "Nicolas Rescher, Editor," even if the instructions in the journal say articles should be addressed only to "The Editor." It is important to know who the editor is and to think of yourself as addressing that person, because editors set styles for their journals. Say nothing more in your cover letter than "Please consider this . . . page manuscript titled . . . for publication in your journal." You do not need to say that it is a comment on an article published in a recent issue or that it is on a subject in an area of the editor's central interest because all of that will be—if you know what you are doing—obvious from the title. Use the departmental stationery from your university. If you are a faculty member, put your title below your name, for example, "Assistant Professor." If you are a graduate student, you don't need to say so; just sign your name. There is, by the way, no prejudice in the profession against graduate students who submit publishable papers.

Publishing is important for two reasons. I have remarked that by publishing you become a member of a professional community of scholars, expose your work to constructive criticism, and thus participate in the lifelong learning process that is the essence of philosophy. But also, if you want to be a professional philosopher, you must publish to get and keep a job in academe (which continues to be the main source of jobs for philosophers).

Thus, painful as it is for some people to face, a practical reason for publishing is to be a contender in the competition for jobs. If you design your term papers to be notes and comments, and the chapters of your dissertation to be articles, by the time you get your Ph.D. you could have a bibliography of three or four publications. You can be sure that many new Ph.D.'s each year will. So let's talk about quality.

It isn't worthwhile to publish just anything just anywhere. You have to produce high-quality work that can be published in the best places. It is a waste of time to publish in student journals, local publications (your university magazine), state academy proceedings, or any unrefereed journal or collection. You get no credit for working your way up in philosophy.

Only performance at the top counts. Consequently, you should aim from the beginning to publish in the most prestigious journals. I am not being quite as elitist as this sounds. Standards in philosophy mostly do not admit of degrees, so it is difficult to publish in any standard journal. You might as well set your goals high because usually only work of high quality gets published.

A traditional way to begin—even easier than writing a discussion article—is to ask your professors if they know any book review editors who might give you a book to review in your area of research. A standard book review format consists of a paragraph summarizing the book's thesis followed by a short critical discussion of a specific point as outlined above. A good, critical book review does not count as much as a note or an article, but it does show that you know what you are doing.

4

WRITING A DISSERTATION

This guide is for people who want to be professional philosophers. Almost the only way in America to make a living as a professional philosopher is to teach in a college or university. To obtain a teaching job in academe, you must earn a Ph.D. And this means that you must write a dissertation.

A. HOW TO CHOOSE A TOPIC

In America today, most dissertations are not so much original contributions to knowledge and scholarship as they are demonstrations that their authors know enough about research and writing to make it likely that they will go on to do some worthwhile work. Many dissertations are thus merely perfunctory and diagnostic, like a set of answers to a Ph.D. comprehensive examination. In most universities you can get by minimally with unpublishable work, but (in my estimation) to do it that way both demeans you and wastes your time. It also provides you with a license to practice a trade for which you are not prepared. You must be able to write publishable papers to obtain and hold a position as a professional philosopher in a college or university. To use your time profitably, and to reassure yourself about your career choice, I urge you to choose an important and serious dissertation topic so that your work is the basis for several publishable articles and a book.

Whatever your topic, you should try to pose your thesis

problem so that the acceptability of your work does not depend on providing a definitive solution. The point, of course, is that you are going to be doing a lot of work on a project that has a conclusion about which you are probably now uncertain, so you want to make sure your work is usable whatever that conclusion is. Even if you set out to find a proof in logic, you may be able to show the philosophical significance even of not discovering the proof.

I recommend that your first article be about thirty manuscript pages long and contain no more than three arguments. An acceptable dissertation could contain five or six such arguments or movements, each requiring thirty or forty pages to develop. Any project that requires more than half a dozen major chapters is bigger than is required and should be set aside for later. Only in special circumstances, for example, in a data-filled dissertation in the history of philosophy, should the work exceed three hundred manuscript pages.

Your dissertation should be complete in itself. That is, you should not choose as a project a problem that is part 1 of a three-part book. If you do have such a grand project in mind, use part of it as your dissertation only if it can be presented complete as a book in itself.

Again, the present academic climate is such that long, total-field dissertations are not required. There is still seen here and there something that used to be known as the Harvard dissertation. It is on the model of European dissertations, consisting of several hundred pages summarizing and criticizing the world literature on the subject, followed by several hundred more pages in which a new contribution in the field is presented. Such dissertations are meant not only to be definitive books; they become the lifework of some scholars who manage to finish and publish them only in their fifties.

What I recommend is a compromise between the dissertation as perfunctory exercise and the dissertation as lifework. You probably cannot succeed as a professional philosopher if your dissertation does not contain at least a competent development of a problem or a point, and you are not using your time most profitably if you do not write a dissertation that can be turned into a book. A timely topic presented in two hundred or three hundred pages will do it.

An apparently obvious way to proceed is to pick your topic and then look for the appropriate professor to direct your dissertation. But it is almost always impossible to do so unless you decide while an undergraduate what you want to work on and where you intend to go to graduate school. Of course, it would be wise of you to do that, but not many of us are that wise. Most likely you will settle your interests only after you have committed yourself to a department by completing most of the requirements other than the dissertation. If you pick a topic on your interests alone, you may not find a professor in your graduate school who can or who wants to direct it.

My recommendation is that you first pick your dissertation director and then look for a dissertation topic with his or her guidance. You will choose someone, of course, whose interests are similar to yours. But you may settle on a topic that is not exactly what you would have chosen by yourself. This is probably all right. Dissertations, after all, are directed. Make sure, however, that your professor understands and approves of your plan to turn the dissertation into a book. Discuss carefully the question of whether or not your project is an appropriate subject for a short book.

Two delicate matters arise in the last paragraph that you will have to work out. The first is that you must have a director who approves of the dissertation-derived book as a contribution to philosophy. Such books seldom contain the definitive statement on a philosophical problem but are often provocative essays in an area of contemporary interest and excitement. They are sometimes quite successful, but young philosophers may hesitate to undertake them either because they cannot adequately isolate a topic from larger issues to round out a conclusion in two hundred to three hundred manuscript pages or because they are afraid to present a topic in preliminary or trial-balloon form, which may be all a young scholar not yet steeped in his subject can manage. These hesitations must be overcome. Young scholars can advance their work and their careers by publishing a short book early, but if they hold back many years to write "the big book," they bury their early work. Granted that dissertations are available from University Microfilms, they do not count as publications and few philosophers regularly look up and read dissertations. The general assumption is that if it is good enough to be published, it will be. The point I am driving at here, however, is that if you are interested in writing a short dissertation in the form of a short book, you must gain your professor's direct support of the project.

The second delicate consideration is that if you want to work, produce, and publish in an orderly and regular fashion, you should choose a dissertation director who does just that. If a professor has published very little or has taken fifteen years to publish his or her dissertation as a book, then it is not likely that this professor is going to view favorably your plan to write a modest dissertation that can soon be turned into a modest book. If you want to publish, associate yourself with a professor who publishes. Then the two of you choose an appropriate topic.

Before you choose a dissertation director, find out from older graduate students which professors conscientiously read students' material immediately and keep to a schedule of discussing it within a week of your turning it in. There are enough temptations to put off your work without adding a sluggish professor to them.

After you choose a dissertation director, go only to that person for advice and discussion. This advice is probably too restrictive, but my concern is that you not confuse yourself by discussing your project with this and that professor, each of whom will have perfectly good ideas, but each of whom will set you on a different course. Stick to one major advisor for unitary and consistent direction.

B. HOW TO WRITE A DISSERTATION

If you can write a discussion note, then you can organize several pieces of that length into an article; if you can write an article, you can organize several chapters of that length into a dissertation. There is, then, no need to be intimidated by the thought of having to write two hundred pages or more. Think about the project enough to organize it into half a dozen parts, and then complete these parts one by one. This is the advice Descartes gave for solving problems: break them down into parts and proceed in sequence.

Begin by going to the library where there is a complete file of dissertations that have satisfied the requirements of your department. Check some of them out and read them both to see how they are put together and to get an idea of what a dissertation project amounts to and of the level on which the work must be done. Look most carefully at those that have subsequently been turned into books.

Two of the chapters are routine, the introduction and the conclusion. In the introduction, you should present the thesis problem by means of a survey of enough of the pertinent literature to provide a solid background for understanding the dissertation. The conclusion should contain a summary of the arguments in the main text, with a specific statement of your major point or position.

Write the introduction first. You may very well revise it drastically once the dissertation is completed, but in the beginning, work on the introduction eases you into the dissertation. If you are not sure about the content or organization of the chapters in the body of the text, writing the introduction will help you get them straight.

There is another reason for writing the introduction first. You may discover in the course of your survey reading that you do not have a dissertation project after all. It is good to find this out early. And if you have been thorough, you can turn the introductory chapter even of an aborted dissertation into a survey article. Before you begin work, you should study survey articles in such journals as *American Philosophical Quarterly* and cast your introductory chapter as much as possible into that form.

Work in the introductory chapter toward a final sentence that begins "Now I turn to . . ." or "Now I examine . . ." or

"Now I argue. . . ." Then bring each chapter to a conclusion that leads into the next chapter. This sequencing leads naturally to a final chapter in which the arguments in the body of the text are summed up in a conclusion that is the point of the dissertation.

Start writing your dissertation as soon as you settle on a topic. Many students make the mistake of trying to read all the pertinent literature before starting to write. You already know something about the topic or you wouldn't have chosen it, so start your introduction on the basis of what you know. Of course, you will have to read background literature and study some texts very carefully to write the dissertation, but write while you do it. Write paragraphs and summaries of the background literature for use in the introduction, and develop arguments and write critical analyses concerning the main texts you are working on as you read them. Sort this material under the chapter headings and organize what you have under each heading into arguments. Again, if you are not quite sure how things are going to develop, you can get ideas and develop chapter plans as you accumulate, organize, and fill in under each chapter heading. The point of writing as you go is to obtain results right from the start. The dissertation will grow as you work on the material, and when you finish all your reading and study, you will have a substantial framework, already partially filled in. If you are exceptionally well organized, you may have an almost fully completed dissertation by the time you finish your dissertation research.

Some people do read all the material first without writing a word, and then with all of it in mind, they sit down to write. If this seems possible for you, then go ahead with it. But writing as you study enhances your thinking and learning about the material. If you are thinking about what to say about something as you are reading it, then you are engaged in the process of critical analysis that is the lifeline of philosophical argument.

Edmund Husserl wrote for hours every day. You are not Edmund Husserl, and it is very hard to maintain a routine of writing every day. Nevertheless, there comes a point when all that really remains is putting together the final draft of your dissertation. You have your basic thesis in mind, and you have read all that is necessary (it is important to know when to quit, and if you don't know, ask your dissertation director). So sit down and write it. If you set yourself a schedule of writing (or putting together from previous material) ten consecutive pages a day, you may not finish ten a day, but in a month you ought to have your first draft virtually completed. This is pretty fast. A more common routine is to arrange to have ten to twenty pages written each week for discussion with your dissertation director.

Whatever system you use, you should strive to finish a complete first draft as soon as possible. Rewriting is wonderfully satisfying when you know that you have a complete draft done. Above all, avoid the trap of rewriting as you go along. It is demoralizing and unrealistic to attempt to revise each page or argument or chapter into near perfect form before you go on to the next. Some students spend years on their first chapters (and seldom finish a dissertation) because they think each part must be perfect before they can go on to the next.

Nothing is perfect. Just as each chapter need not be perfect before you go on to the next, the dissertation itself need not be the last word on the subject at hand; it need be only satisfactory. Professors often seem to be so exacting and so knowledgeable that students sometimes fear to show them any work at all. If you begin to worry excessively (to the extent that you can't write or won't show your professor your work when you complete it for fear that it isn't good enough), you can regain your sense of proportion by reading a few more dissertations. In particular, if you are intimidated by your dissertation director, get *his* or *her* dissertation on interlibrary loan or order a copy from University Microfilms and read it.* Of course, some

*University Microfilms International (300 North Zeeb Road, Ann Arbor, MI 48108) has available for purchase most of the Ph.D. dissertations that have been accepted by American universities in recent years.

dissertations are very good, but few of them are as fabulous as the mythical model some paralyzed students have in mind.

Give a complete draft of your dissertation to your director as soon as you can. After he or she has gone over it with you, strive to revise it according to his or her instructions as well as you can. You do not have to do everything recommended, but you should have good reasons if you reject any of your director's major suggestions. Walk a line between two extremes. You might actually know as much as or more than your dissertation director does about the subject you are working on, but there is no reason for you to reject all suggestions, just as there is no reason for you to accept all suggestions even if you think your director is a much better judge of your work than you are yourself. Keep in mind that it is your dissertation.

It is even more important to retain your own sense of what your dissertation is meant to show after your director has accepted it and a draft has been passed around to your committee. You are almost certain to find that one of your committee members has the impression that you were attempting to write a dissertation different from the one you have presented, and you may be inundated with advice about how to turn your dissertation into something that it is not. If your dissertation director is satisfied with your original draft, then you can be confident in your polite presentation of reasons why you do not want to change the thrust of entire sections, or add new sections, or even use the same material to write a different dissertation. It is tactful to make some alterations suggested by each member of your committee, but you must recognize that it is highly probable that you cannot make all the changes suggested by all the committee members without contradictory results. You have to figure out how far you can go with each. The fact is that some professors who make suggestions even for extreme changes will barely glance at your revision. If you make a point of telling them what you have revised on the basis of their comments, this is usually enough. You understand that I am assuming that none of them has turned up a basic contradiction or has provided a demonstration that your conclusion does not follow or hold.

Once all the members of your committee have read your draft and made suggestions, work night and day to revise the dissertation to place it in your director's hands just as soon as possible. Try to have the final draft ready within a month. The longer you let it sit, the larger will loom the problem of revising it. Everyone wants to get it over with once your director has approved a draft, so get it done.

5

YOUR FIRST BOOK

Work on something else for six months after you finish your dissertation. But don't let any more time than that pass before you start working on it again. Look for phrasing and material that is present only because of dissertation requirements; revise and cut accordingly. Shape the text into a book manuscript and see what you have.

Your greatest temptation will be to take several years to expand the manuscript into a larger and more complete work than you have in hand. Certainly, this is sometimes the right thing to do. If you have followed the plan outlined in this guide, however, you will already have a short, well-circumscribed book manuscript. Work to complete that manuscript within its own boundaries, not to expand it. I have already cited several reasons for turning your dissertation into a publishable book manuscript within a year after you get your Ph.D. One of the strongest reasons is the confidence and status early book publication will give you. Just as writing is a way of thinking, publishing is a way of benefiting from the thinking of others who will read, appreciate, and criticize your work.

Then, of course, practically speaking, the best way to secure a job in a college or a university is to publish a book. Half a dozen excellent articles might do it, but a well-received book is better. The fact is that you probably need two books. It is more and more taken for granted that you will turn your dissertation into a book. So do it as soon as possible in order to have a maximum amount of time (perhaps five years) to finish a second book before you come up for tenure. Again, excellent articles may be enough, but they will have the widest influence and be most useful all around if you plan them as chapters of a book. This is what the most highly respected and influential contemporary philosophers do.

The best, that is, the most prestigious and professionally respectable, place to publish your book is with a select group of university and trade presses. Check with your professors for the names of those presses that specialize in your area. Also look at the book advertisements in philosophy journals, in the American Philosophical Association *Proceedings and Addresses*, and in the *APA Shopping List*. The best way to get your book considered carefully by a press is to have a dissertation director who is respected by editors and who will bring your manuscript to their attention. If you submit the manuscript on your own, find out who the philosophy editor is, call that editor and discuss the manuscript with him or her, and then send it in if the editor wants to look at it.

Do not publish your book in an unrefereed series. Do not pay to have your book published yourself. This is a very difficult subject because today even some of the best university and trade presses require subventions for the publication of books. Perhaps your university will provide the subvention, or perhaps you can get a grant from some foundation for it, and if it is a respected press, there is no stigma attached to your providing the subvention yourself. But again, it will not help your professional career and may even harm it to publish in a series or with a publisher who will publish any manuscript that comes in as long as the author pays for it. Some of these outfits even advertise that they have all manuscripts refereed, and probably they do; but as Hume might have said, isn't it likely that they will take your money and publish your book whatever the referees say? Your colleagues in the profession will know, and they will tell the dean when you come up for tenure.

6

NOTES ON PHILOSOPHICAL WRITING

Philosophical writing is technical writing. Philosophy is, among other things, the art of making distinctions. Philosophical analysis consists of clarifying meanings. Logic is a matter of being consistent in what you say. Neither last nor least important, what you say and how you say it has ontological and epistemological implications. Philosophers should be aware of these implications.

Consequently, in their writing, philosophers must be careful about the meanings and uses of words and other symbols in ways that may appear to be odd or excessively fussy or even cranky. The care philosophers take with words and other symbols is bound to get them into conflicts with stylists, ordinary grammarians, editors, and typesetters. Know not only what you are saying but also why you say it the way you do, and then *if it does make a logical difference*, make them print it your way. (If it does not make a difference, then take Descartes's advice and follow local conventions.) With such thoughts in mind, I present here three short discussions of points in writing that should engage a thinking philosopher, very roughly categorized under the headings "Reason," "Clarity," and "Argument." These lists are by no means complete. They are, as we say in philosophy, paradigmatic. Once you get a feeling for it, carry on. And if you don't? Alas.

A. REASON

1. Criteria

Here are some criteria for good philosophical writing: precision, clarity, logical continuity and consistency, pertinence, and economy. Whatever you do, be consistent. Consistency is of the essence of argumentative philosophy.

2. Hypostatization and Personification

Something that always amazes me about philosophical writing is the use of stylistic conventions that imply the hypostatization of entities that the philosophers doing the writing would never on their lives allow in their ontologies. Thus, you find Goodmanite nominalists saying such things as "Constructivism insists that Platonism is false" as though both constructivism and Platonism were real. Moreover, the sentence implies that constructivism is the kind of entity that can insist. Another common example of such false personification is the paper that begins "This paper will argue that only human beings can use language." If that is true, then surely it is the case that the paper—not being a human being and thus not being capable of using language—is not going to do any arguing. At the end of the same paper, of course, you will find the conclusion "This paper has shown that only human beings can use language." So if you do not believe that collective entities are substantive or conscious, then look carefully for the intentions and purposes of the particular thinking individuals hidden in such statements as "Think not what your country can do for you, but what you can do for your country." At least avoid attributing demands, intentions, and mental lives to entities not commonly thought to have minds. There is only one possible response to sentences such as "Locke's theory of real essence states that . . . ," which is: *Really*?!

(Perhaps you believe that your nominalist credentials are such that you have earned the right to use collective nouns, personification, and the like in apparently ontologically compromising ways because everyone knows that such modes of speech are reducible to nominalistic terms and that you don't really mean it. Shouldn't you be allowed some liberties of style to liven up tedious topics? Not if you want to avoid misunderstanding.)

3. Dangling Participles

Philosophers alert to avoiding hypostatization and personification should never have problems with dangling participles. For example, "Walking down the street, the morning was beautiful" leaps out and smites any philosopher's sensibilities, for any philosopher knows that a morning is not the sort of entity that walks down the street. "Walking down the street, I saw that the morning was beautiful" is correct.

4. Which and That

There is philosophical precision in using 'which' and 'that' correctly:

> 'which' introduces a nondefining (nonrestrictive) relative clause.
> 'which' does not limit; it gives a reason or adds a new fact or refers to the denotation of the antecedent in general.
> 'which' is correct if "in general" is meant.
>
> 'that' introduces a defining (restrictive) relative clause.
> 'that' identifies the person or thing meant by limiting the denotation of the antecedent.
> 'that' is correct if the question "Which one(s) in particular?" is appropriate.

What philosophical difference does it make if you do not use 'which' and 'that' correctly? A philosopher, if anyone, should be interested in the fact that there is a standard grammatical way of indicating the difference between defining and nondefining relative clauses. Big trouble can arise from not being clear whether or not a phrase describes a defining characteristic of a subject.

But how do you decide whether or not a relative clause is defining or nondefining? Must a defining characteristic or condition be necessary, sufficient, or both necessary and sufficient? Is it material, causal, logical, conceptual, or even accidental, or some combination of these? You decide. You are the author. Use the criterion or criteria appropriate for the circumstance, and then indicate your decision with proper use of 'which' and 'that'. Your use of 'which' and 'that' indicates to your readers what *you* take to be defining and nondefining relative clauses, and it implies the criterion or criteria you follow in making the distinction.

If all this leaves you reeling, there are two rules of thumb that do not work in all cases but are helpful:

> 'which' is correct if the sentence still sounds right when you put a comma after the word preceding 'which'.
> 'that' is correct if the sentence still sounds right when 'that' is left out.

5. Spell It Out

For the quoting convention used in discussing 'which' and 'that' in note 4, see note 22, "Use and Mention." And while you are there, after the first occurrence of the phrase 'word or term or phrase' in the first sentence of note 22, substitute the word 'it' for the second occurence of that phrase. This example shows why I used the phrase throughout, and not 'it'. Here I follow a rule always followed by G. E. Moore: spell out what you mean.

The word 'it' is vastly overused. For example: "Nor does it imply that his parents are capable of creating his soul." Here 'it' means "their production of his body" and so should be replaced by the words 'their production of his body'. Watch for these cover words. Sometimes it is even hidden from the writer. (In the last sentence 'it' means "exactly what is meant" and so should be replaced by the words 'exactly what is meant'.) Sometimes 'it' covers up the fact that you do not know what you mean. When you do figure out what it all means, substitute a short descriptive phrase for 'it'.

Now substitute the word 'this' for the word 'it' in the preceding paragraph.

Similarly, avoid 'former' and 'latter' whenever possible by putting instead a short descriptive phrase indicating which is meant. Do not make the reader look back. And try not to use 'etc.' or 'and so on'. If there is something more to say, say it. (Some people try to support arguments with 'etc.' Consider: "All the top authorities agree with me, including the Father, the Son, and the Holy Ghost, etc.")

6. Generality and Specificity

Never use a general term when you mean something specific. Never use a vague term when you mean something specific. Never use an ambiguous term when you mean something specific. These three rules seem hard for some people to grasp. Never use a term at a level of generality higher than the level of specificity on which your comments or arguments apply. In general, be specific. Consider: "If an idea is of this particular sort, then. . . ." The particular sort here is that meant by the words 'clear and distinct', so say: "If an idea is clear and distinct, then. . . ."

7. Like

When you say, for example, "A philosopher like Quine would say . . . ," make sure that you mean "A philosopher similar to Quine" and not Quine himself. If you do mean Quine himself, then say, "A philosopher such as Quine would say. . . ."

8. Can, Could, May, Might

In the sentence "One may interpret 'x' to mean . . . ," do you mean that one has permission to do it or that one has

the ability to do it? Probably you mean that one can do it.
Consider:

> "One *can* interpret 'x' to mean . . ."
>   if one has the ability to do so.
> "One *could* interpret 'x' to mean . . ."
>   if circumstances were right.
> Something *can* or *could* take place
>   if it is possible.
>
> "One *may* interpret 'x' to mean . . ."
>   if one has permission to do so.
> "One *might* interpret 'x' to mean . . ."
>   if one were so inclined.
> Something *may* or *might* take place
>   if it is likely.

9. Only

Put the word 'only' next to what it modifies. The British
always put the word 'only' as far from what it modifies as
possible, for example, "There only was in Descartes's ontol-
ogy, which actually had three substances divided between
finite and infinite, the latter of which is self-created, mind and
matter." This sentence illustrates the standard problem of the
British placement of 'only'. Just what does 'only' modify in
the sentence? Consider another example: the literal meaning
of "Philosophers only seek the truth." This means that they
only seek it: they never find it, shun it, deny it, or regret it,
all of which options are left open by "Philosophers seek only
the truth." (But of course this last sentence suggests that they
never seek anything else, which is patently false.)
    Test case:

> Only I know that I am a thinking thing.
> I only know that I am a thinking thing.
> I know only that I am a thinking thing.
> I know that only I am a thinking thing.
> I know that I only am a thinking thing.

I know that I am only a thinking thing.
I know that I am a thinking thing only.

10. Both . . . And . . .

Do not use 'both . . . and . . .' to link two elements of differing sorts or orders. To do so is to make a category mistake. "Both dogs and cats" is OK, but not "This is both false and would make the search for truth unnecessary," which links a passive with an active mode.

11. Hopefully

'Hopefully' is an adverb. It is used to describe how some action is performed, as are the adverbs 'awkwardly' and 'rapidly'. If you mean "I hope", then say so.

When you say "Hopefully we may conclude that . . . ," one presumes that you mean "I hope to conclude that . . ." but probably you mean "I conclude that . . .", which is the best way to say it. False modesty has no place in philosophy. If you only hope that you might have a point, then there is no point in setting it down. Is there any relation between this misuse and the adverbial theory of sense perception? (Is the last question a joke? See note 50, "Jokes.")

12. Continuous Present

Philosophical ideas and positions and opinions are usually best stated in the continuous present tense. Use the past tense only when you are referring to something as actually past. Consider, for example, the sentence "Descartes's position was that ideas were modifications of the mind." Now it is true that that was his position, but because he is a great, grand philosopher, it still is and ever will be his position. Furthermore, his position is not that ideas were modifications of the mind, but that they are: "Descartes's position is that ideas are modifications of the mind." Obviously, however, "On the morning of 11 February 1650, Descartes was very ill." But, "Even though he was ill, he knew that two plus two is four."

Tenses can cause some difficult problems. Philosophers, after all, change their minds. If you are discussing actual time sequences, and what a philosopher once held but no longer holds, then use the past tense. But even then the idea itself is in the continuous present: "Formerly, Descartes held that he might be deceived in thinking two plus two is four; later he changed his mind." (But does the use of the continuous present imply the subsistence of eternal Ideas in Plato's Realm of Being?)

13. He and She

English does not contain a full complement of distinctive neutral and collective pronouns and generic terms. Thus, the generic terms 'man' and 'mankind' may mean either "all men exclusive of women" or "humankind". To convey your meaning precisely, you should reserve the generic term 'man' for reference only to men and use 'humankind' when you mean to refer to all men and women together. You should, however, be careful to apply this rule neither anachronistically nor in such a way as to give a false interpretation of a philosopher's beliefs and intentions. In Western philosophy a considerable number of discourses on man are biased toward men. It might not be misleading to speak of humankind in discussing Locke's conception of man, but it is incorrect to so translate Nietzsche. The best rule here is to discuss a philosopher in that philosopher's own vernacular, making such explanatory comments as you deem necessary to the understanding of that philosopher's position.

The fact that 'he', 'his', and 'him' can be used to make reference either to a man or to a woman also leads to imprecision. To be perfectly clear, you should reserve these terms for reference to men only and use 'he or she', 'his or hers', and 'him or her' when you mean either or both neutrally. Also, because 'she', 'hers', and 'her' are not generally used to refer to either men or women or both neutrally, it is confusing to use them in place of or as a variant of 'he', 'his', and 'him' in the neutral sense. The general point is that in cases where there is ambiguity and thus possibility of misinterpretation in common usage, philosophers concerned with being understood exactly should adopt the precise primary usage of the terms and not use them neutrally.

Because the repeated use of such phrases as 'he or she', 'his or hers', and 'him or her' seems cumbersome to some writers, they suggest that new collective or neutral pronouns be introduced into English. But no philosopher should eschew necessary repetition at the expense of clarity of expression. New technical terms are often useful, but such terms as 's/he', 'his/hers', 'him/her', and other compounds have not caught on and are no less cumbersome than are the ordinary expressions they are meant to replace. Beyond that, English is spoken as well as written, and philosophy papers are often read aloud. A compelling argument, then, for employing 'he or she' rather than 's/he' is that 'he or she' disrupts the train of speech less than does 's/he' and also is universally understood without readers having to learn the meanings of new technical terms. Also, the presence of unusual terminology distracts readers' attention from meanings to the forms in which these meanings are expressed.

The possessive 'their' should not be used with a singular subject. For example, "Any person using this machine is responsible for their own mistakes" is grammatically incorrect and should read "Any person using this machine is responsible for his or her own mistakes." Of course, in this case one could say, "Persons using this machine are responsible for their own mistakes." But when no ready way to avoid the use of 'he or she' or similar locutions is apparent, use them. (Excellent writers, for example, Shakespeare, do sometimes use 'their' with singular subjects. The guideline in philosophical writing, however, is not what sounds best but what conveys meaning clearly and unambiguously. It is best to use 'they', 'their', and 'them' consistently only for plural reference, and 'he', 'she', and 'it' consistently only for singular reference. One way to avoid possible confusions is to use key words univocally.)

Overall, the problems of conveying generic, collective,

and neutral meanings in English without ambiguity can be solved simply with the use of grammatically correct ordinary English expressions, and should be.

14. Jargon

Philosophers use a lot of jargon. You have to decide whether or not it is useful. For example, if you use 'fact of the matter', 'interanimation', or 'supervenient', you have to be sure your readers know what you mean, or you have to give explanations. It is usually best to avoid jargon.

Plugging jargon into your sentences is like plugging a component into your computer. It does your thinking for you. (*Does* it?) Consider what George Orwell says about the use of ready-made phrases: "They will construct your sentences for you—even think your thoughts for you, to a certain extent—and at need they will perform the important service of partially concealing your meaning even from yourself" ("Politics and the English Language," 172). Jargon is thus related to clichés. Try to avoid clichés. I think I shall throw up if I find another red herring, straw man, Aunt Sally, or hare in my philosophical soup.

15. Empty Words

In a similar vein, avoid empty words. Here are some: 'important', 'relevant', 'crucial', 'interesting', and 'significant'. What is important, relevant, crucial, or interesting? Why? How is it significant? Be explicit.

16. Rules

Remember, rules are made by mortals like you and me. We can't follow them all the time, and only fools try to. But if we don't follow some rules most of the time, nobody will know what anyone is saying. Consider Cratylus's paradox. Because he thinks everything changes all the time, he fears his words will change their meaning as he speaks them and he will be misunderstood, so when spoken to he just wiggles his finger. But what does he think people will make of that?

17. Categorization

You disagree with the way I categorize these notes? Good, you have the makings of a philosopher. As an intellectual exercise, why not categorize them your way? (If my teasing-teacher style gives you a pain, is that a reason for discounting what I say?) Start by figuring out why I list the items of group C under 'Argument'.

B. CLARITY

18. Rewriting and Criticism

Writing is mostly rewriting. Give your manuscripts to colleagues to comment on. If they disagree with you, all the better. You want the most severe criticism you can get. You must rewrite to avoid those criticisms.

Then after all that work, you will send the manuscript in and it will be rejected because some referee misses your point. He or she must be an idiot, you think, to misunderstand something that is so crystal clear. But it is more likely that the text seems clear to you because you understand so well what you want to say. You know what your words mean because you know what you intend them to mean. But your reader does not get your point. So now you have to rewrite to put your arguments in words that mean to your reader what they mean to you.

Here is the hardest thing to learn: do not be personally sensitive to criticism. Being criticized is part of being a philosopher. Every criticism is based on something you have said. Coolly and calmly figure out what the basis of each criticism is. How did the reader get that mistaken idea from your words? Even if you find the misinterpretation ridiculous, mean, or just plain off the mark, you should rewrite to avoid the criticism or misunderstanding. The burden is on you, the

writer, to communicate your thoughts clearly. Almost every
mistaken interpretation is in part the writer's fault. Ask for
criticisms, welcome them, and then rewrite to stifle them.

19. Spelling and Meaning

Write with a dictionary at your elbow for two reasons.
You should check the spelling of every word about which you
are uncertain, and you should check the meaning of all words
that you intend to convey a precise meaning.

My weak spelling has been the bane of my professional
life. Perhaps I don't pay enough attention, but for whatever
reason I have to look up the same words time after time. And
I never catch them all. You absolutely must use the dictionary.
(The standard publishing dictionary is *Webster's Ninth New
Collegiate*.) No matter how good your arguments are, readers
are going to smirk and think you an illiterate ignoramus if
you misspell common words. If you have spelling problems,
always carry a pocket dictionary. Use the spellcheck if you
write on a word processor.

The misuse of words is insidious. Because philosophical
issues often revolve on very subtle distinctions of meaning,
you must always be careful to get your words just right. Are
rights and duties *reciprocal* or merely *mutual*? Is your conclusion an *inference* or an *implication*? Is your point *confirmed* or
proved? Some philosophers even seem confused about
whether Descartes *doubts* or *denies* that he has knowledge.
Look it up.

Writing without a dictionary is like climbing walls in Yo-
semite without ropes. Do it long enough and you will make a
bad mistake.

20. Proofreading

Proofread your manuscripts. What impression can you
imagine you are making on peers, professors, or editors if you
give them material that they read more carefully than you do?
I know it's hard; I'm a terrible proofreader myself.

21. Univocality

If you define 'soul', then use 'soul' univocally throughout, and do not for the sake of varying a monotonous style toss in 'spirit' and 'mind' now and then. Unsystematic shifting among vaguely synonymous words is very confusing.

22. Use and Mention

In philosophical writing, it is often important to indicate whether you are using a word semantically to refer to its meaning or are mentioning or referring syntactically to the word itself. The standard logical convention is as follows: Put the word in double quotes when you are using it to refer to its meaning; put the word in single quotes when you are mentioning it to refer to the word itself. The convention is designed to show that exactly the same set of typographical marks indicates meaning when surrounded by double quotes but indicates merely the marks themselves when surrounded by single quotes. Thus, 'dog' usually means "dog", but if you wanted to use 'dog' to mean "cat", this quotation convention makes it possible for you to explain precisely that you are doing so.

Notice that the punctuation is outside the quotation marks in the above example. Editors who do not understand the reason for this convention will try to get you to put the punctuation marks inside the quotation marks, so you must explain carefully to them the reason for the convention. It is a technical use of quotation marks developed by logicians. In logic, 'x.' is not the same sign as 'x'; "x." means something different from "x".

Practically speaking, of course, nothing crucial hangs on the difference between 'dog' means "dog", and 'dog' means "dog," but when the word and not its meaning is in question, you must write "dog" is expressed by 'dog', and not "dog" is expressed by 'dog,' because as is obvious, 'dog,' is one set of typographical marks and 'dog' is another.

23. Contractions

Use contractions only in direct quotations of speech. Words such as 'not' and 'are' have strong uses in philosophical discourse. Give them their due. (Then why have I used contractions throughout this text? Because this guide is written informally in a familiar mode of speech. It is not so much argumentative as advisory or suggestive. See also note 16, "Rules.")

24. Dashes and Colons

The use of a dash in place of a colon is common, but a colon is designed for the purpose of setting something off firmly: one such symbol is enough. The dash is useful as parentheses within parentheses, as in "A three-in-one entity (the Trinity—Father, Son, and Holy Ghost—is an example) is. . . ." Under the general logical principle of using one sign in one way, one should restrict the use of the dash.

25. For

Many sentences beginning with 'For' are not complete sentences. Either hook the clause onto the last sentence by putting a comma instead of a period and changing 'For' to 'for', or delete 'For' and start the sentence instead with some phrase such as 'If so . . .'.

26. Double-Spacing

Double-space everything. This format makes everything easier to read. Editors and typesetters demand that everything be double-spaced. The word 'everything' in the last sentence means "everything". I have instructed students to double-space everything who later say in surprise after I have corrected their papers, "Oh, you mean quotations, footnotes, and bibliography, too?" 'Everything' means "everything". And do not have your typewriter or word processor justify the right margin of your manuscript, leaving uneven spaces between words. This handling makes the manuscript hard to read and can lead to serious typesetting confusions. Furthermore, in precise philosophical writing, shouldn't spaces of different width between words logically mean different things?

27. References

In general, give full references as I do at the end of this book. In particular, put your references in the form used by the journal or press you are submitting to (some of which do not require full references).

28. Be Brief

To learn how, read *The Elements of Style* by Strunk and White.

C. ARGUMENT

29. We

The use of 'we' in the polite sense, as in "We have now seen . . . ," "We have argued . . . ," "We now turn . . . ," and so on is a rhetorical device that might be calculated to draw the reader in. Consider the reader who responds, "Not me, buddy! Speak for yourself. You and me don't form no we." There are similar problems with 'our', as in "Our concern now is. . . ." *Is* it *our* concern?

30. I and You

Readers are interested in Descartes's intellectual biography of discovery, but not in everyone's. There are two discovery styles of writing. One is from the viewpoint of the author. "I came across this problem while reading . . . when I saw . . . and, I had an idea that. . . ." The other is from the viewpoint of the reader: "You will see that . . . as you saw a moment ago . . . as you will agree. . . ." These are sometimes

threaded together with the we-style: "We shall find . . . and
then we shall see. . . ." As I remark above, the we-style
annoys some readers, as does the I'm-taking-you-by-the-
hand-(you nitwit)-and-guiding-you-through style. Only popes,
kings, and presidents can get away with the we-style these
days. You are writing the paper, so say: "I show that . . . I
argue. . . ." (Nicholas Rescher argues that the I-style is egotis-
tic. In philosophy we allow for differing opinions.)

The other extreme is to speak of yourself in the third
person. This would seem to be excessively modest, for example, "The humble author of this paper begs to suggest the
tentative opinion that. . . ." You mean "I argue that . . .", so
why not say so? If you do not, one might get the impression
that you mean "I claim without argument (or with an inadequate argument) that. . . ." (Note the use of 'one' as a cover;
one can say, "One gets the impression that this is nonsense,"
when one actually means, "I am quite sure this is nonsense.")

If you really are so uncertain as to have to hide behind
such screens as "this would seem to be . . ." rather than "this
is . . ." or "the writer thinks that . . ." or "we are of the opinion that . . ." rather than coming right out with "I argue
that . . ." (not "I am trying to say . . ." but "I say . . . ," for a
mere try isn't good enough), then are you sure you want to
expose your inadequate claims to criticism?

31. Space and Time

There is also a question of whether to place your paper
and your message in space or in time. In time: "I will show . . .
as I showed a moment ago . . . and will show later on. . . ." In
space: "As I show above . . . and as I show below . . . and as
I show in this paper. . . ." Are you showing it *now* or *here*?
The temporal sequence style goes along with the discovery
style. I recommend the space style. The paper is in the reader's
hands and the entire argument is there on the paper. You
have put the words on paper. If you say, "I will show . . . ,"
you are not actually referring to what you will show, for you
have already put it on paper; you are referring to the reader's

voyage of discovery and really mean "You will see. . . ." But maybe the reader will not see.

How can you say that the argument is on a piece of paper when all that is on the piece of paper is a batch of black marks? Is that hypostatization? That aside, if you place your message in the continuous present and in space, you are not quite so likely to make curmudgeons complain that you are trying to draw them in as you will if you use the past tense in time.

(Note how much comprehension of that last sentence depends on your very careful attention to and memory of what has gone before. I really should rewrite it to make clear what I mean, which is that "we have seen . . . " may be false and "you will see . . . " remains to be seen. Many people think that, for example, G. E. Moore's concern to spell everything out in complete detail is excessive and derogatory of his readers' intelligence. It is certainly possible to explain something in too much detail, but being misunderstood because you say too little is worse.)

32. Title

Provide a title descriptive of content. "A Note on Plato" is inadequate. What about Plato is the note about? If you cannot think of a good descriptive title, you may not know exactly what your paper is about.

33. Conclusion

Do not end with a rhetorical question. State your conclusion.

34. Grand and Extraneous Comments

You must put your point in context, but grand comments about the course of Western philosophy, the opinions of Heidegger or Quine, or the spirit of the age are out of place, are diversionary, and may expose your ignorance. Extraneous comments put in to fill space are to be avoided for the same reasons. In philosophy, never say more than is necessary to make your point. (Is this last sentence necessary? Try to avoid unnecessary repetitions.)

35. Province or Focus

Be precise about the province or focus of the point you are making. Is it a strongly formal point? Does it have a defensible formal expression? Or is it a pragmatic suggestion? Is it useful? Is your point stipulative, or is it an empirical or a logical discovery? Do you mean to be edifying? If you stray beyond the boundaries of the province, you'll probably get in trouble. Knowing where you are is sometimes difficult, but it is necessary if you are going to write in a unified and consistent way.

36. Hedgehog and Fox

In short papers, don't try to be a hedgehog who knows a big thing grandly; be a fox who knows a little thing well. Limit yourself to what you can handle. If you take a modest topic and stick just to it, you will avoid accusations of ignorance or lack of philosophical aptitude.

37. Audience

Decide for whom you are writing. How much do they know about the background? If you use Quine, decide whether or not you are operating within Quine's theory. If you are, is your exposition technical enough? And does it go beyond what he says or implies? If it is just an application of a Quinean point, then for whom? If it is for philosophers of social science, then you have to defend Quine. If it is for social scientists, then you have to explain Quine.

38. Language

For serious work, you have to learn the language. Greek for Plato, Latin for Aquinas, French for Descartes, German for

Kant, Logic for Quine. (Jargon for journals?) What language is required for Heidegger?

39. Sarcasm

The temptation to be smartass or sarcastic is great in philosophical writing. It has never won a logical argument yet. (Here is a proposed counterexample: A speaker was pontificating about how a double negative makes a positive, but a double positive never makes a negative. From the back of the room came Sidney Morgenbesser's world-weary voice, "Yeah, yeah.")

40. Not

Just as an exercise, rewrite the following sentence to avoid any problems with the use of 'not': At least do not have entities not commonly thought to have minds running around making demands.

41. A, B, and C

In logic, 'a, b, and c' means something different from 'a, b and c', or, more precisely, as yet (they are in single quotes) these symbols mean nothing, but because there is a syntactical difference in their form, there should be a difference in their semantical use. Here is an example: Remington, Smith, and Wesson make guns. Three gun makers. By contrast, the answer to the request "Name two gun makers" might be "Remington, Smith and Wesson." It is British style to do without the comma before the 'and' in a sequence of three or more terms, and this use is becoming common in the United States. If it helps any, that comma is known as the Harvard serial comma, from an old Harvard style manual. It means something.

42. Ellipses

Three dots mean continuation; four dots include the period at the end of the sentence. If you delete part of the inside of a quoted sentence, use three dots to indicate the deletion. If your deletion starts in the middle of one sentence and takes up again in the middle of a succeeding sentence, use four dots to indicate that the quotation is a composite of two sentences. Now here is a problem: If the deletion starts in the middle of one sentence and takes up in the middle of the fifth sentence farther on, should you put seven dots to indicate the number of sentences in between? Most people seem to think indication of whether the deletion is within one sentence (three dots) or extends to another sentence (four dots) is enough. What, however, would you make of this one? Descartes says "ideas are. . . . images" (footnote: pp. 12–37).

43. Lists

When categorizing things in a list, beware the urge to make it come out to some nice round number. Also curtail the impulse to suppress an item in a categorized list merely because it unbalances the list with an odd number. But speaking of odd numbers, note the popularity of groups of three. Why is it that so many things seem to us to have three parts? Trinitarianism? Beginning, middle, and end?

44. Craft

Writing philosophy is a craft, like carpentry. Different pieces are designed to fit different places.

45. Hopes, Wants, and Wishes

"I hope to show in this paper . . . ," "I want to show in this paper . . .," and "I wish to show in this paper . . ." all should be replaced with "I show in this paper. . . ." If all you can manage is a hope, want, or wish, forget it. Obviously, this point bears repeating.

46. More

'More' is a comparative. When you say that something is more this or more that, always answer the question, "More this or that than what?"

47. Since and Because

'Since' is commonly used in the sense of "because", particularly by English philosophers, but because 'since' can also mean either "from a definite past time until now" or "subsequent to a certain past time and before the present", such phrases as 'Since it happened' are ambiguous. Does the writer mean something temporal or something causal? When you mean "because", it is best to use 'because'.

Why is 'since' so popular? The reason is that the "because" meaning of 'since' is weaker than the "because" meaning of 'because'. Test the strength of your conviction that you mean "because" when you use 'since' by changing the 'since' to 'because'. You will be surprised how often you are not so sure about what you are saying when you use 'because' instead of 'since'. Even if you do continue to use 'since' in the sense of "because", it is a good exercise and test of your convictions to see how 'because' sounds in the sentence.

48. Then and Therefore

Surely you can make this one up yourself. "Is he really serious about this?" you ask. Sure, if and when it makes a philosophical difference. You decide when the temporal sense of 'then' conflicts with the nontemporal sense of 'therefore'.

49. Jokes

If you have a lively sense of humor, you'll probably get in trouble now and then in writing philosophy. Nothing is more easily misunderstood than a well-crafted joke. For example,

I've broken most of these rules in this very text. Is that a joke, or am I just following note 16, "Rules"?

You should be careful that your jokes are not misunderstood, and you must watch to make sure whether or not the philosopher (David Hume? Nelson Goodman?) you are reading is joking. How can you tell? It is important to know because some very influential philosophical writings turn out to be jokes.

50. Revision

That reminds me of the joke about the young person who asked an old person on a street corner in New York City how to get to Carnegie Hall. The old person fixed the youngster with a steely eye and said: "Practice! Practice! Practice!"

If you want to publish: "Revise! Revise! Revise!"

7

CRITIQUE OF A DISCUSSION NOTE

In this section and the next I give critiques of two of my own papers, comparing what I had in mind when writing them with how successful they seem now. A referee of this guide said that this choice is in bad taste because it is immodest and self-glorifying. But if that were true, then wouldn't my writing this guide itself be an even more egregious example of putting myself forward? So what is one to do?

One must learn to criticize the work of others because a large part of philosophical writing consists of such criticism. But equally important—and usually more difficult—is attaining the ability to criticize one's own work. Professional writers must be able to step back and criticize their own writing dispassionately in order to revise and improve it. My examples are meant to help you learn this skill, and if you notice some failures in my analyses that favor me, so much better the lesson.

I wrote the first draft of "Rules of Inference in Stephen Toulmin's *The Place of Reason in Ethics*" for a seminar in ethics given by Professor William K. Frankena at the University of Michigan in 1958. Several years later I revised and cut it to the discussion note reprinted here.

The topic of Frankena's seminar was contemporary ethics. We examined the three hottest books then going in ethics: R. M. Hare, *The Language of Morals* (1952), P. H. Nowell-Smith, *Ethics* (1954), and Stephen Toulmin, *The Place of Reason in Ethics* (1950). It was a wonderful seminar. Frankena himself gave me the idea of writing my term paper as a discussion note by remarking that Professor Paul Henle used to teach a course in contemporary philosophy in which the requirement for a passing grade was the publication of a discussion note on some topic being debated in the current journals. This was a good way, he said, to begin publishing. Frankena's own career had got off to a roaring start with his publication of a brilliant critical discussion of a crucial point in G. E. Moore. Why couldn't I do the same?

I should say immediately that three reasons why fame didn't follow my paper are that it isn't as good as Frankena's, Toulmin didn't reply to it, and finally Toulmin's work in ethics is not as important as that of G. E. Moore. So another rule in picking a point or book or philosopher to criticize is to try to fasten onto one that is going to be of lasting importance. Some philosophers do have the knack.

Rules of Inference in Stephen Toulmin's
The Place of Reason in Ethics

> *Paragraph 1.* In his analysis of the use of moral terms Toulmin finds that moral reasoning follows a pattern different than, e.g., that of the syllogism. Specifically, he finds that what might be taken as premises in a syllogism operate as rules of inference in moral reasoning. Having carefully pointed out that the principle of harmony acts as the supreme (second level) rule of inference for arguments justifying subordinate (first level) rules of inference which in turn justify arguments for particular moral conclusions as to action, Toulmin goes on to say that any other *way* of reasoning is not moral reasoning. Toulmin expresses this by saying that the use of any other supreme rule of inference than the principle of harmony defines another realm of reasoning activity than that of morality.

Paragraph 1 of my note is a good précis of the thesis of Toulmin's book. But it strikes me now that unless you have been steeped in the principles of mathematical logic and ideal language philosophy, you may lack the background required for getting all that is implied in this paragraph. For example,

I assume that the reader knows that sentences can be taken either as premises or as rules of inference depending on how you set up your logical system. The notion of different language games for different realms is still current.

Spare as this first paragraph is, it is adequate because a discussion note is meant for readers who know the subject well. The first paragraph provides orientation.

> *Paragraph 2.* It is clear, then, that it is not specifically the *pattern* of reasoning which distinguishes moral reasoning from other kinds, but the content of the supreme rule of inference. One might generate the pattern Toulmin has discovered as follows. Take any syllogistic pattern, e.g.,
>
> > All *A* are *B*.
> > All *B* are *C*.
> > All *A* are *C*.
>
> according to which one can argue that if an *A* is *B* then it is *C*. Rewrite this syllogism as a rule of inference, roughly,
>
> > If *A* is *B*, and *B* is *C*,
> > this is a good reason for deciding that *A* is *C*.

A pattern of reasoning with such rules can be set up syntactically with no concern whatsoever as to content. If Toulmin had claimed that this *pattern* uniquely distinguishes moral reasoning, he would have opened the door to moral relativity. Toulmin effectively distinguishes moral reasoning from other kinds by indicating the content of the supreme rule of inference (which justifies all arguments for the contents of subordinate rules of inference in the system). Prudential reasoning might have the same syntactical pattern as does moral reasoning, but the content of its supreme rule of inference is different than that of morality. Hence, Toulmin does not open the door to moral relativity, at least in no ordinary sense. Though the variables may be interpreted in various ways in various societies, the content of the supreme rule of inference remains the same. Therefore, Toulmin's discovery of the way of moral reasoning includes the discovery both of a pattern of reasoning and the content of the supreme rule of inference.

In paragraph 2, I narrow my exegesis of Toulmin's position, stressing that Toulmin does not distinguish moral reasoning solely by the pattern he has uncovered, but by this pattern in conjunction with the content—harmony—of moral reasoning's supreme rule of inference. This exegesis in fact goes further than Toulmin may have wished to go. But I strive to hold him to it by arguing that the overall pattern of reasoning could be the same both for moral reasoning and for prudential reasoning, which would differ only in the content of their supreme rules of inference, harmony for morality and prudence for prudentiality. I also try to hold him to this position by arguing that unless moral reasoning is defined by the content of the supreme rule of inference, moral relativism—which I presume Toulmin wants to avoid—will result.

> *Paragraph 3.* I am concerned with the conclusiveness or justification of Toulmin's discovery of the content of the supreme (second level) rule of inference in morality. Not denying that Toulmin has discovered a pattern and a content, I question whether the *way* he has gone about it justifies his claim to have discovered *the* way of moral reasoning. I contend that Toulmin's way of investigating (moral) reasoning is a third level of argument (third level way of reasoning) which uses a third level rule of inference, the content of which is controversial. It may be that Toulmin *has* discovered the way of moral reasoning, but to the extent his findings derive from a controversial method of investigating ways of reasoning, to that extent his findings are inconclusive (or unjustified).

In paragraph 3, I state my criticism, for which I assume the apparatus of meta-ethics, which again requires that the reader have knowledge of ideal language philosophy. My claim is that Toulmin must justify his assertion that he has discovered *the* way of moral reasoning by appealing to a higher-level way of reasoning. My criticism is that the supreme rule of inference for this higher level is controversial. But I notice that in fact I swallow my main point here. That if the rule is controversial it has not been established is so obvious to me that I assume that it will also be obvious to the reader, and thus I fail to state it explicitly. This is a bad but common failing in a lot of philosophical writing.

Readers should by now have recognized that I am raising the old Pyrrhonian skeptical problem of the criterion. Many of them could go on to complete my argument themselves, to the conclusion that Toulmin's method leads either to a vicious circle or to an infinite regress.

> *Paragraph 4.* An outline of the three levels of argument under discussion will allow me to make my point precisely.

> III. *Third level philosophical rule of inference*:
> If a principle is generally accepted as *the* supreme rule of inference in a realm of reasoning, this is a good reason for deciding that this principle *is* the supreme rule of inference in that realm of reasoning.

>> 1' ' '. *Factual premise*:
>> The principle "If a rule tends to maximize harmony and minimize conflict in society, this is a good reason for deciding to use this rule as a rule of inference for drawing particular moral conclusions" is generally accepted as the supreme rule of inference in moral reasoning for drawing conclusions about rules of inference to be used in particular cases of moral reasoning.

>> 2' ' '. *Philosophical conclusion*:
>> The principle "If a rule tends to maximize harmony and minimize conflict in society, this is a good reason for deciding to use this rule as a rule of inference for drawing particular moral

conclusions" *is* the supreme rule of inference in moral reasoning for drawing conclusions about rules of inference to be used in particular cases of moral reasoning.

II. *Second (supreme) level moral rule of inference*:
   If a rule tends to maximize harmony and minimize conflict in society, this is a good reason for deciding to use this rule as a rule of inference for drawing particular moral conclusions.

   1' '. *Factual premise*:
      Using the rule "If one makes a promise, this is a good reason for deciding to do what one promised" as a rule of inference for drawing particular moral conclusions tends to maximize harmony and minimize conflict in society.

   2' '. *Moral conclusion*:
      The rule "If one makes a promise, this is a good reason for deciding to do what one promised" *should* be used as a rule of inference for drawing particular moral conclusions.

I. *First level moral rule of inference*:
   If one makes a promise, this is a good reason for deciding to do what one promised.

   1'. *Factual premise*:
      I promised to return this book.

   2'. *Moral conclusion*:
      I *should* return this book.

I need not expand upon the controversial nature of the third level rule of inference. Since Toulmin's method implies the third level argument, it is clear that the conclusiveness of his findings rests upon accepting the third level rule. Until Toulmin can establish this third level rule of inference, he cannot claim (by his present method) to have conclusively discovered the supreme rule of inference in any way of reasoning.

In paragraph 4, then, I show three levels of reasoning—philosophical, moral (general), moral (practical)—and point out that they all depend on the establishment of the philosophical level.

> *Paragraph 5.* I have called this third level a philosophical level for two reasons. First, one might wish to establish the third level supreme rule of inference by finding that it is generally accepted by philosophers. This, of course, would not be to establish the rule, but to assume it. If one attempted to escape this circle by proposing a fourth level of argument, one would be on the way to an infinite regress.

Of course the third, philosophical level never appears in Toulmin's book. I argue that it is there implicitly and that its need of justification vitiates Toulmin's claim to have discovered *the* pattern of moral reasoning. So in paragraph 5, I suggest that the need for justification may lead to an infinite regress.

> *Paragraph 6.* The second reason for calling the third level philosophical is that Toulmin seems to imply that the principle of harmony *should* be the supreme rule of inference in moral reasoning. If this is implied at all, the third level of argument could then be outlined as follows:

> III. *Third level philosophical rule of inference:*
> If a principle is generally accepted as the supreme rule of inference in a realm of reasoning, this is a good reason for deciding to use this principle as the supreme rule of inference in that realm of reasoning.

> > 1′ ′ ′. *Factual premise:*
> > The principle "If a rule tends to maximize harmony and minimize conflict in society, this is a good reason for deciding to use this rule as a rule of inference for drawing particular moral conclusions" is generally accepted as a rule of inference in moral reasoning for drawing con-

clusions about rules of inference to be used in particular cases of moral reasoning.

2' ' '. *Philosophical conclusion*:

The principle "If a rule tends to maximize harmony and minimize conflict in society, this is a good reason for deciding to use this rule as a rule of inference for drawing particular moral conclusions" *should* be used as the supreme rule of inference in moral reasoning for drawing conclusions about rules of inference to be used in particular cases of moral reasoning.

I hesitate (on Toulmin's grounds) to call this third level "should" moral, so I call it philosophical. (I do not believe it is logical.) Toulmin would probably reject this version of the third level argument, but there is a hint of it in his book. If it *were* proposed, one might wish to investigate the difference between the moral "should" and the philosophical "should". One might wish to inquire how one goes from a philosophical rule and a factual premise to a philosophical conclusion (a similar problem occurs on the lower levels in deriving moral conclusions as to action from moral rules and factual premises). And finally, now one could seriously discuss the relation between levels in terms of successively higher levels justifying (in various senses, perhaps) succesively lower levels. One might very well be led to ask for a justification of the third level argument, which, as in the first version, could lead either to a circle or an infinite regress, in this case, of "shoulds".

In paragraph 6, I expect the reader to know about the problems of deriving moral conclusions from factual premises. But here I am doing too much in two ways. My contraposing of philosophical and moral "shoulds" is not entirely cogent. Nor is it fair of me to impose this contraposing on Toulmin and then say that *I* am not sure about the distinction. By this I mean to imply that *he* is not cogent about the distinction, but he could throw up his hands and say that I have gone far beyond anything he has said or would say, so why should he reply? And indeed he did not.

The second way I let this note get out of hand is by trying to do too much. I try to make two points, one about the infinite regress, the other about the movement from factual (or philosophical) premises to moral conclusions. The "should" problem does lead to the vicious circle that is the companion of the infinite regress in elaborations of the criterion problem, but here it is obvious that the superstructure I lower over Toulmin's claims is not substantial enough to shake them.

Nevertheless, the application of the criterion problem to Toulmin's text is a good idea, and I still believe that the criticism exposes a serious problem. How *does* Toulmin justify his procedure?

Today I would grade this discussion note A for zeal and for being on the right track, B for execution, and C for relevance.

8

CRITIQUE OF A JOURNAL ARTICLE

For a number of years I could raise my blood pressure by reading the most recent book on Descartes. Most Cartesian scholars are apparently committed to defending Descartes. This means that they have to get through the First Meditation and on to the Sixth without being stopped by Descartes's skepticism. Because I agree with such early critics as Pierre Daniel Huet that Descartes's skepticism is so stringent that he cannot get out of it, I decided to write a paper showing that according to his own method of doubt, Descartes can know nothing at all. That gave me the title: "Descartes Knows Nothing."

(I had forgotten, but after I wrote this critique I came across an old term paper in which I argue that on Descartes's principles you can doubt your own existence. I wrote the paper for an undergraduate course given by Richard H. Popkin in 1950 at the University of Iowa. Thirty-four years later a draft was published as an article, and three years after that a revised version was published as a chapter in a book. Perhaps, then, an appropriate subtitle for this discourse on writing would be "Waste Not.")

The title is very important. "Descartes Knows Nothing" is a good title because it encapsulates the thesis and conclusion of the paper, and it is catchy. It also starts a reader thinking: What do you mean, "knows nothing"? And what do you mean by 'nothing'? A solid title like this can give a writer a lot of confidence. I was sure I knew what I had to say.

I analyze below the paper "Descartes Knows Nothing" in some detail, both from a writer's viewpoint and from a reader's viewpoint, more or less paragraph by paragraph. I give my reasons for doing what I do and then also provide objections to my procedure. In this way I do what Jack W. Meiland recommends about argumentative writing in his *College Thinking*: give arguments, but also provide objections to those arguments. In an argumentative paper you should raise and meet the main possible objections to your position. I do not always do that here because often the question is moot. There are numerous ways to construct a philosophical paper. I am illustrating only one way.

Someone might, then, object to the title "Descartes Knows Nothing" on the ground that it is flippant. Also, it states the conclusion of the paper but does not indicate its context, content, or form. How about "Descartes's Method of Doubt Leads to Skepticism"? All right, but it is not pithy. I counter that "Descartes Knows Nothing" does give a hint of skeptical goings-on, and despite my saying that you should be open with your readers, you have to tease them some to keep their interest. And I give it all away in the first paragraph, anyway.

Descartes Knows Nothing

Paragraph 1. The defense of reason is crucial in maintaining the viability of Cartesian metaphysics because philosophers who take seriously Descartes's admonition "to meditate seriously with me" often find it impossible to reach that "certain and evident knowledge of the truth" that is Descartes's stated goal.[1] There are doubts that Descartes can know anything at all. I contend with these critical philosophers that the First Meditation embeds Descartes so deeply in agnosticism that he can know neither that anything exists, nor, supposing he could know that something exists, what any existing thing is. Descartes is bereft of knowledge both of the existence and of the essence of anything. I conclude that Descartes knows nothing.

Footnote 1. "Preface to the Reader" in *Meditations on First Philosophy*, tr. by Haldane, Elizabeth S. and G. R. T.

Ross in *The Philosophical Works of Descartes*, Vol. I (Cambridge: Cambridge University Press, 1931), p. 139.

The editor of *History of Philosophy Quarterly* (where "Descartes Knows Nothing" was published) does not require an abstract, but it is a good idea to give one anyway so readers can decide whether or not they want to read your paper. My first paragraph, then, is almost an abstract of the paper. What it does not contain is an outline of my arguments. The first paragraph also winnows out readers. It is obvious that I am writing for people who know something about Descartes and Cartesianism. I assume that they catch the allusion, for example, to the fact that in the *Meditations*, Descartes first claims knowledge of his own existence and then goes on to ask if he does not then also know his essence.

Paragraph 2. I mean three things by 'nothing'. First, 'nothing' means empty of cognitive content. Thus, in "What Moves the Mind? An Excursion in Cartesian Dualism,"[2] I argue that Descartes's innate ideas of mind, matter, and God are vacuous. Descartes's major innate ideas—of thinking, of extension, and of necessary existence—are empty of content, and in this sense Descartes knows nothing of these universal essences.

Footnote 2. Watson, Richard A. "What Moves the Mind? An Excursion in Cartesian Dualism," *American Philosophical Quarterly*, Vol. 19 (1982), pp. 73–81.

Paragraph 3. Second, my arguments may suggest that Descartes opens the door on being as nothingness. Perhaps Descartes knows nothing in this existential sense, but I do not develop that possibility here.

Paragraph 4. Finally, the primary sense in which Descartes knows nothing is that he knows no thing, neither in essence nor in existence. It is in this failure to know particular things in the world that Cartesian metaphysics breaks down.

In paragraph 1, I state my thesis. In paragraphs 2, 3, and 4, I answer a question that I assume readers will ask: What do you mean by 'nothing'? This is difficult, because nothing is a big topic in philosophy. Do I define the term 'nothing'? No, I assume that readers know the ordinary meaning of 'nothing', but I do indicate this ordinary meaning in paragraph 2 by relating nothing to emptiness. I say that Descartes knows nothing in the sense that his ideas are empty of cognitive content. I do not argue this point in "Descartes Knows Nothing," so I make reference to a paper in which it is argued. It happens that I wrote the paper cited, but in a situation where you want to begin with a position that has already been argued, you might very well cite a paper written by someone else.

One could object that it is bad policy to begin a paper by citing another that readers ought to read first. I agree, but I am trapped. I have to specify the important case of knowing nothing in the sense of having an idea that is empty of content, both because it is a major sense and because it is important in my argument about Descartes. However, I am writing a short paper and cannot say everything in it. So I give the citation and rush on, hoping for the best. I do indicate for knowledgeable readers that my argument about ideas is based in part on Descartes's claim to have innate knowledge of "Platonic" ideas.

In paragraph 3, I indicate that I am aware that Descartes's *cogito*—in which existence is known before essence—is in the background of the existentialist thesis that nothingness underlies being. I skip quickly over the abyss.

In paragraph 4, I give the main sense of 'nothing' that is pertinent. Descartes knows *no thing*. I considered using 'no particular thing', but that construction interferes with the move from "nothing" to "no thing", so I stayed with the hope that readers would see that I mean "no particular thing". This distinction comes out later, anyway.

> *Paragraph 5.* The question of existence is metaphysically less crucial than the question of essence. The denial

that Descartes can know even that he himself exists, however, appears to be counter-intuitive, so I begin by examining Cartesian reasons for doubting whether anything exists. Then on the assumption that external objects do or can exist, I argue that Descartes cannot know what they are.

Paragraph 6. That is, I take the metaphysically significant sense of "Descartes knows nothing" to be the claim that even if he knows that something exists, he cannot know what that thing is. So we could give Descartes knowledge of the existence of things. And the point of doing so would be just to show the cognitive vacuity of mere knowledge of existence. A thing of which one knows no characteristics, but only that it exists is known no better than if it were uncharacterized. What is uncharacterized is nothing, so to know nothing of a thing's characteristics is little better than, if not the same as, to know nothing.

Always try to anticipate your readers' questions. In paragraph 5, I assume that readers are resisting because everyone knows that the one thing Descartes proves absolutely is his own existence: *Cogito, ergo sum.* So I try to disarm the readers by saying that despite their probable inclinations, existence is much less important than essence. But I assure them that I will look into the matter. Now I notice that I don't fulfill that promise very well.

More important is what things are; this is usually what we mean when we say we know something. So in paragraph 6, I come to the crux of the matter. I argue that Descartes cannot know what anything is. Here I use a standard argumentative ploy. As Gustav Bergmann said to me once about a paper I had written for him as a graduate student, "Goddamn it, Watson, philosophy is done with an epée, not a broadsword." So you give your critic every possible advantage and then win your point with an elegantly restrained thrust that draws only the required single drop of blood. In the present case, if Descartes is given knowledge of existence but is shown to have no knowledge of essence, suddenly he finds himself empty-handed. This is the main argument of my paper. Knowledge of uncharacterized existence may lead to existentialism, but it certainly is not knowledge of something.

Paragraph 7. The slippage of language in this last sentence leads to a crucial question, as old as Plato: Can one know that something exists without knowing what it is? Descartes obviously claims that knowledge of the existence of something can be independent of knowledge of its essence. Given this separation, Descartes attempts to make two moves generally thought to be impossible or illegitimate in philosophy: from existence to essence and from essence to existence.

Paragraph 8. Using the *cogito* as foundation, Descartes claims to go from knowledge only of the existence of something to knowledge of what that thing—a thinking mind—is. And in the ontological proof, Descartes tries to go from knowledge only of the essence of something to knowledge that that thing—God—exists. I argue that Descartes fails in these attempts. But more than that, even if he could go from one to the other, after the First Meditation, Descartes can have knowledge of neither essence nor existence of anything.

My argument is a bit slippery—does the move from 'nothing' to 'no thing' not need defense?—so I indicate that I know it does, but I let it stand and go on to point out that Descartes tries to make two traditionally illegitimate moves, from existence to essence and from essence to existence. Again, I say I can give Descartes these moves and still conclude that he cannot even begin because he can know neither existence nor essence to begin with.

I

Paragraph 9. In the First Meditation, Descartes proceeds through several stages of doubt that can be ordered as follows:

1. External things exist with characteristics such as color and shape, and in relations such as cause and effect, but because of the possibility that my senses and reason might provide incorrect reports about these things' sensory and conceptual modes, I cannot know for certain that the external things I am now perceiving and conceiving are as I perceive and conceive them to be.

2. External things exist with sensory and conceptual modes, but because of the possibility that these modes are different from the sensory and conceptual modes through which I perceive and conceive these things, I cannot know for certain that the external things I am now perceiving and conceiving are like my perceptions and conceptions of them.

3. External things exist with characteristics such as color and shape, and in relations such as cause and effect, but because of the possibility that I may be hallucinating or dreaming, I cannot know for certain that the perceptions and conceptions I am now having are of external things that exist.

4. External things might or might not exist with sensory and conceptual modes, but because of the possibility that God, a demon, or I myself might be the cause of the perceptions and conceptions I am now having even if no external things exist, I cannot know for certain that any external things exist at all.

Paragraph 9 contains an outline of Descartes's progressive stages of doubt culminating in complete skepticism about the existence of external things. My implicit claim is that this analysis—an ordered presentation in terms of increasing removal from primary assumptions about external things and the sensory and conceptual modes through which we perceive and conceive them—represents the true argument of Descartes's First Meditation. Now just how does one argue for such an analytical model? In a dissertation, you might spend a chapter showing line by line how you derived your model from Descartes's text. There is not room for that in a short paper. But should I not argue somehow for my model? In cases like this, everyone goes by the convention that the paper has been approved by an editor and some referees. This approval does not mean that they agree with or stand behind everything in the paper, but at least they think it is professionally competent. The writer then is trusted to present a summary model of this sort as well grounded. In fact, I worked as long on this model to make sure that it is logically and textually accurate as I did on any other section in the paper. It is open to challenge and might be criticized by someone in a discussion note. It is the sort of thing a beginning philosopher might fasten onto as a subject for critical comment.

> *Paragraph 10.* In summary, if I assume that I have knowledge that an external thing exists, and of the properties of external things in general, then I can doubt (1) that I have correct knowledge of its properties, (2) that I have any knowledge of its properties, and (3) that I am perceiving and conceiving it or any existing thing. Then if I doubt both that external things exist and that I know their properties in general, I can doubt (4) that I am perceiving and conceiving any existing thing at all. Descartes takes these arguments to be conclusive concerning the dubitability of knowledge of both the existence and essence of external things.

The numbered outline is logically complete, but it is difficult to read, so in paragraph 10, I summarize it. The summary does not contain the argument but frames it for readers.

> *Paragraph 11.* In the First Meditation, Descartes also casts doubt on reason. In parallel with the above stages, even if I assume that my reasoning processes are generally reliable or consistent, I can still doubt ratio-

nal inferences because (1) sometimes I make mistakes and have lapses of memory, (2) the relations among existing things may differ from representations of them by reason, and (3) reasoning while hallucinating and dreaming may be of nonexistent things. Finally, (4) because of the possibility of the demon, I can doubt that I am reasoning about any existing things at all. Descartes later substantiates this fourth possibility by insisting on a voluntaristic God Who can create things whose descriptions are contradictory to our reason, or that we cannot conceive of without contradiction.[3]

Footnote 3. "He determined Himself towards those things which ought to be accomplished for that reason, as it stands in Genesis, *they are very good*; that is to say, the reason for their goodness is the fact that He wished to create them so. . . . Again it is useless to inquire how God could from all eternity bring it about that it should be untrue that twice four is eight, etc.; for I admit that that cannot be understood by us. . . . Hence neither should we think *that eternal truths depend upon the human understanding or on other existing things*; they must depend on God alone, who, as the supreme legislator, ordained them from all eternity." "Reply to Objections VI," Haldane and Ross, Vol. II, pp. 250–251. The concept of a square circle is contradictory to our reason; I cannot conceive of my own nonexistence without contradiction.

In paragraph 11, I want to say the same thing about reason that I just said about sensory knowledge. I have already indicated this parallel by including conceptual modes in the model, so now I can summarize in 1–2–3–4 fashion to conclude that just as I do not know whether or not I am sensing any existing thing, also I do not know whether or not I am conceiving or reasoning about any existing thing.

The last sentence of paragraph 11 is what is known as a throwaway line. In philosophy, you have to allow your opponent some assumptions, and this is what I am doing when I say that I can give Descartes knowledge of existence and still prove that he knows nothing. Here I have established that the First Meditation leads to complete skepticism. Then I remind any objector that later on Descartes says that human reason and even the principle of contradiction can be transcended by God, so how can you still be defending human reason?

I do not argue explicitly for the throwaway line. Instead, I provide a quotation from Descartes in footnote 3 to establish the point. Throughout the paper I give extensive quotations from Descartes in footnotes to support my thesis and so readers can see immediately the passages on which I base my interpretation.

You should not put any substantive commentary in a note that can be incorporated in the text. If a comment cannot be incorporated in the text, then you must have a very good reason for putting it in a note. Some authors indulge themselves excessively by putting in notes everything that occurs to them as they write the text. This may illustrate their cleverness and erudition, but it destroys the consecutive flow of the argument and tends to drive readers frantic. You do not want your readers puzzling or worrying all the time as to why you included this or that note. I do allow myself a substantive comment in footnote 3 as an expansion of Descartes's text. It is unnecessary.

"Descartes Knows Nothing" has an unnumbered introduction and seven numbered sections. Should the sections have short descriptive subheads? Yes. Why did I not provide them? It is a short paper. I resent too much guidance myself and resist explaining everything to readers. I think roman numerals are aesthetically more pleasing alone. I got bored. I was lazy. I should have given subheads.

II

Paragraph 12. What happens if these reasons for doubt are taken seriously? First, consider the fallibility of memory. In his *Censura philosophiae Cartesianae*, Pierre Daniel Huet attacks Descartes by insisting on the activity or discursiveness of all thinking, even of those thoughts expressing simple relations.[4] Huet suggests that as an argument, the *cogito* cannot be expressed as "I think, therefore I am," but rather in some such form as, "I think, therefore I was," or "I think, therefore I will be," or "I thought, therefore I was," or "I thought, therefore I am," or "I thought, therefore I will be," but never "I think" and "I am" in the same moment. The two members of all of the above expressions are different thoughts separated in time. The conclusion of any argument is always dubitable because, as Descartes himself admits, discursive reasoning is dependent on memory which is not trustworthy from moment to moment.

Footnote 4. Huet, Pierre Daniel. *Censura philosophiae Cartesianae*. Campis: Caspari Cotii, 1690.

What kind of paper is this? It is a history of philosophy paper, but it is in a journal open to what is called analytic history of philosophy, papers about the history of philosophy with as much or more logical argument about doctrine as material about historical connections and influences. I wrote the paper for the *History of Philosophy Quarterly*, stressing analytical points. In paragraph 12, I link a traditional argument to a historical figure, Pierre Daniel Huet. Notice that I do not quote Huet, nor do I give page references in footnote 4. I could have done so, but my purpose here is not so much to be exact about what Huet says as to develop his argument logically. Thus, I am accurate to Huet's logic but not literally accurate to his words. Is this approach bad? Not for my analytic purposes. Had the paper been submitted to the *Journal of the History of Philosophy*, however, the editor would have made me be explicit about what exactly Huet said. I would already have done that had I been writing the paper for the *Journal of the History of Philosophy*. As it is, even though I am a former editor of that journal, I am quite sure that this version of "Descartes Knows

Nothing" would have been turned down by *Journal of the History of Philosophy* as not historical enough.

> *Paragraph 13.* Descartes very soon denies that the *cogito* is an argument.[5] The *cogito* may be expressed in the form of an argument, but when pressed Descartes claims that he knows his own existence by intuition. Every momentary act of thinking that I exist—even that of doubting it—involves the apodictic certainty that I do exist.[6] Descartes thus tries to save knowledge of his own existence by eliminating a dubitable discursive argument and basing certainty on instantaneous intuition.
>
> *Footnote 5.* "When we become aware that we are thinking beings, this is a primitive act of knowledge derived from no syllogistic reasoning. He who says, '*I think, hence I am, or exist*,' does not deduce existence from thought by a syllogism, but, by a simple act of mental vision, recognizes it as if it were a thing that is known *per se*." "Reply to Objections II," Haldane and Ross, Vol. II, p. 38.
>
> *Footnote 6.* "I am, I exist, is necessarily true each time that I pronounce it, or that I mentally conceive it. . . . I am, I exist, that is certain. But how often? Just when I think." "Meditation II," Haldane and Ross, Vol. I, pp. 150–151.

Paragraph 13 contains a point all students of Descartes know, but I need it, so I try to make it brief. I fill it out with footnotes. Notice that I give the quotations here in English from the Haldane and Ross translation. For the *Journal of the History of Philosophy*, I would have given the quotations in Latin or French; if in French, say, I would have then given full references to the Latin and English versions. In my book *The Breakdown of Cartesian Metaphysics*, where "Descartes Knows Nothing" is the last chapter, I give all the quotations in French. Last chapter of a book? Surely you do not think I wrote "Descartes Knows Nothing" *just* as a journal article, do you?

Check over your footnotes again and again. It is difficult enough to support a philosophical position without exposing yourself to the accusation that you are depending on a misquotation or a statement that is not to be found on the page you cite.

When you give a quotation that has been translated into English, check carefully to make sure that it is an accurate translation from the original language. It is embarrassing to build an argument on a mistranslated passage. However, sometimes the English translation may obscure what you take to be crucial. In such a case, you can provide your own accurate translation.

> *Paragraph 14.* Elsewhere, however, Descartes claims that we can grasp arguments atemporally and thus avoid the doubts attendant on discursive reasoning. He urges us to practice intuiting even extensive arguments all at once, in a single intuition.[7] Thus even if the *cogito* were an argument, we could intuit the truth of "Everything that thinks exists; I think; therefore, I exist." Fallible memory is foiled.
>
> *Footnote 7.* "Rule XI. *If, after we have recognized intuitively a number of simple truths, we wish to draw any inference from them, it is useful to run them over in a continuous and uninterrupted act of thought, to reflect upon their relations to one another, and to grasp together distinctly a number of these propositions so far as is possible at the same time. For this is a way of making our knowledge much more certain, and of greatly increasing the power of the mind.*" *Rules for the Direction of the Mind*, Haldane and Ross, Vol. I, p. 33.
>
> *Paragraph 15.* Alas, a problem remains. Suppose the *cogito* is not an argument. Eliminate 'therefore'. We still have a complex proposition, "I think, I am." In the instantaneous intuition of this proposition we still must grasp the relation between "I think" or a thing that is thinking, and "I am" or a thing's existence. Descartes himself admits that reason can be deceived in its comprehension of the relations of com-

patability or logical connection even of two simple ideas intuited at the same moment. So whether the *cogito* is either an argument or merely two related concepts, grasping it intuitively does not guarantee its truth.

In paragraph 14, I raise an objection to my steamroller push toward skepticism. Maybe knowledge of existence is intuitive. But in paragraph 15 (we could surely do without the unctuous "Alas"), I counter with the fact that the *cogito* is a complex proposition. Even in the intuitive grasp of a relation between only two elements, you might be deceived. So I can round out the conclusion with a nice "either-or."

> *Paragraph 16.* Thus, when thinking and thinker are put in relation—discursively or logically—this attribution of relation can then be doubted either by challenging memory required in following an argument, or by challenging reason required in recognizing logical connection. That is, even if memory were trustworthy, I can doubt that a thinker exists because I could be wrong about the relation between thinking and thinkers. And this on two levels: Acts may generally imply actors, but I could be mistaken in this specific case. On a deeper level—think of the Eucharist[8]—God may have created this act without an actor, this property without a supporting substance, this thinking without a thinker.

> *Footnote 8.* Watson, Richard A. "Transubstantiation Among the Cartesians" in Lennon, T. M., J. M. Nicholas, and J. W. Davis, eds. *Problems of Cartesianism*, Kingston and Montreal: McGill Queen's University Press, 1982, pp. 127–148.

Is paragraph 16 necessary? It just repeats what has already been said. This is a technique professors use in lecturing: tell them what you are going to say, say it, and then tell them what you have said. There is some place for in-other-words repetition in philosophical writing, but try to avoid it when you can. In this case, readers surely suspect me of setting it up so I can get in a reference to my own paper on transubstantiation. They would be right. And, you know, the *Citation Index*—something the dean will check when you come up for tenure to see how often your published works are cited in the literature—does not distinguish between citations of an author's works in an author's own papers and citations in papers written by others. (I blush to say that this obvious point never occurred to me until a colleague pointed it out.)

> *Paragraph 17.* Moreover, even supposing there is a thinker, how do I know that this thinker is I? Again I could be mistaken, or God could have done what is contradictory to our reason but is not impossible for God, acquaint me with some thinking that appears to be mine but really belongs to another, or even to no one at all.

> *Paragraph 18.* Because the thinker is separate or distinguishable from the thinking, one can know neither that something is thinking nor who is thinking. Hume was by far not the first to look within and not find himself. Descartes cannot know that the thing whose existence and essence he thinks he knows is himself.

Paragraphs 17 and 18 are my entrées in the contest for elegant, packed brevity. Paragraph 17 refers back to the arguments about mistakes and God's voluntarism in linkage with the model argument in paragraph 9 about knowledge of external things. Paragraph 18 carries on with an allusion to Hume, with a first statement—almost swallowed—of the conclusion in "Descartes Knows Nothing" that is most difficult to support: that one cannot know even oneself.

> *Paragraph 19.* Following the arguments above, I conclude that by the time Descartes asks "qu'est-ce donc que je suis?" and discovers that he is "Une chose qui pense,"[9] he has gone far beyond the limits that serious consideration of his reasons for doubting experi-

ence and reason demand. Even supposing that Descartes knows that something exists, to assert what this something is, that it is a mind or soul or self or thinking thing, is to claim to know how it is characterized, and Descartes himself has forever put a gulf between our representative perceptions and conceptions on the one side, and the true nature of the things that may or may not exist on the other side. Two philosophers who take him seriously on this are Locke and Kant. They see that even if the *ego* is an internal thing, it is still external to the perceptions and conceptions representative of it. Another who sees this is Descartes's deviant disciple, Malebranche, who deduces as a major implication of the First Meditation that the essence of mind—like the essence of body—is unknown unless and until revealed by God.[10]

Footnote 9. "But I do not yet know clearly enough what I am, I who am certain that I am. . . . What of thinking? I find here that thought is an attribute that belongs to me; it alone cannot be separated from me. . . . I do not now admit anything which is not necessarily true: to speak accurately I am not more than a thing which thinks, that is to say a mind or a soul, or an understanding, or a reason, which are terms whose significance was formerly unknown to me. I am, however, a real thing and really exist: but what thing? I have answered: a thing which thinks. . . . But what then am I? A thing which thinks." "Meditation II," Haldane and Ross, Vol. I, pp. 150–153.

Footnote 10. Malebranche, Nicholas. "XIe Éclaircissement. Sur le Chapitre septième de la seconde Partie du troisième Livre. Où je prouve: Que nous n'avons point d'Idée claire de la nature ni des modifications de notre âme." Rodis-Lewis, Geneviève (ed.), *Oeuvres de Malebranche*, Vol. III, Paris: J. Vrin, 1964, p. 163.

Paragraph 20. Descartes cannot know that he exists because this knowledge depends on either experience,

memory, or reason, all dubitable according to (1),
(2), (3), and (4) above; nor can he know what he is,
for ultimately this depends on trust in the verisimili-
tude of an idea of mind, which is most thoroughly
ruled out by argument (4). The crux of Huet's objection is that the setting of two notions in relation is
both discursive and complex, and if discursive then
memory can fail, and if complex then reason can
fail. "I think" and "I am" are distinct notions; the
cogito is thus a dubitable proposition; thus I can
doubt my own existence.

Beginning writers often have a tendency to swallow their
conclusions because they are so intent on them that they forget
that their readers are not quite sure what these conclusions
are. Thus, you may state your argument in detail and conclude
with the obvious, "That's it!" and find your readers asking,
"That's what?" So in paragraph 19, I bring readers up to the
present point again, and then in paragraph 20, I provide a
numbered guide to my arguments showing that one can doubt
one's own existence. But I'm beginning to overdo it.

III

Paragraph 21. Is there a way out? It certainly is not
through what must be one of the most difficult discursive arguments in the literature, Descartes's attempted demonstration that clarity and distinctness
are the criteria of certainty.[11] This argument is valid,
but as also in the case of Arnauld's circle,[12] it is
clearly ingenuous if not illegitimate to use reason to
establish criteria to be used in turn to certify reason
when reason itself is in doubt. Does Descartes forget
his reasons for doubting reason? No. I think Descartes expects to be saved by intuition.

Footnote 11. "Certainly in this first knowledge there is
nothing that assures me of its truth, excepting the
clear and distinct perception of that which I state,
which would not indeed suffice to assure me that
what I say is true, if it could ever happen that a thing

which I conceived so clearly and distinctly could be false; and accordingly it seems to me that already I can establish as a general rule that all things which I perceive very clearly and very distinctly are true." "Meditation III," Haldane and Ross, Vol. I, p. 158

Footnote 12. "The only remaining scruple I have is an uncertainty as to how a circular reasoning is to be avoided in saying: the only secure reason we have for believing that what we clearly and distinctly perceive is true, is the fact that God exists.

"*But we can be sure that God exists, only because we clearly and evidently perceive that; therefore prior to being certain that God exists, we should be certain that whatever we clearly and evidently perceive is true.*" Arnauld, Antoine, "Fourth Set of Objections," Haldane and Ross, Vol. II, p. 92.

Where does one start a new section? Where one has to pause to take a deep breath. Beginning section III, I am ready to meet an objection again. Descartes himself apparently uses reason to establish the legitimacy of reason. On his own principles, this strategy just will not work.

Paragraph 22. Consider: If the existence of God is assured by discursive argument, then it can be challenged on grounds of possible memory failure. But suppose we know God's existence by intuitive grasp of an argument or logical relation all at once. Then it can be doubted on the possibility that reason is relating two items—God and existence—incorrectly. This possible error can be avoided, however, if, as in the ontological proof, God's existence and his essence are identical.[13] Descartes would have to argue that here one does not see that two items are related, but rather that one intuits a single, simple idea. God's essence is existence. In connotation, to know the idea of God is equivalent to knowing the idea of necessary existence. In denotation, the idea of God refers to a necessarily existent thing. If I have an idea of God, then I know that He exists. But what is He? He is existence, necessary existence. And if the equation of identity holds, one cannot in this instance argue that it is impossible or illegitimate to go from knowledge of essence to knowledge of existence or vice versa. They are the same.

Footnote 13. "I clearly see that existence can no more be separated from the essence of God than can its having its three angles equal to two right angles be separated from the essence of a [rectilinear] triangle. . . . existence is inseparable from Him. . . . For is there anything more manifest than that there is a God, that is to say, a supreme Being, to whose essence alone existence pertains?" "Meditation V," Haldane and Ross, Vol. I, pp. 181–183. Descartes does not here say explicitly that God's essence is identical with his existence, but when Arnauld says of God that *"because He is an infinite Being . . . [His] existence and essence are identical"* ("Fourth Set of Objections," Haldane and Ross, Vol. II, p. 92), Descartes agrees that "in God essence and existence are not distinguished" ("Reply to the Fourth Set of Objections," Haldane and Ross, Vol. II, p. 113). Also, in reply to Gassendi's objection that existence is not a property or perfection ("The Fifth Set of Objections," Haldane and Ross, Vol. II, pp. 185–187), Descartes says, "God *is* His existence" ("The Author's Reply to the Fifth Set of Objections," Haldane and Ross, Vol. II, p. 228).

Paragraph 23. But Descartes fails even here. The idea we have of God could be without referent, deceptively emplaced by the demon or by God Himself. We could intuit God's existence and simply be deceived, even if our reason informs us that it is a contradiction to conceive of a nonexisting God. Again, to intuit God's necessary existence, Descartes must equate His perfection with His existence. Then if the idea of His perfection includes any content other than that He exists—for example, that He is not a deceiver—the idea of God would be complex and thus dubitable because of possible confusions of reason.

Paragraph 24. Finally, suppose that we accept the proof of God's existence. If the idea of God is merely the idea of existence, even necessary existence, is it not vacuous? Sheer existence is without character, and thus is unknowable as a thing. Existence is not a thing. As remarked above, I argue for the emptiness of content of Descartes's idea of existence in "What Moves the Mind?" And it seems to me that it is fair to say that to know the mere existence of God is to know nothing.

Paragraph 22 contains another objection to my argument. Descartes says that the essence of God is His eternal Existence; that is, existence and essence are the same, so the argument that you cannot go from one to the other does not hold. I meet this objection in paragraph 23 by bringing up the deceiving demon. Then in paragraph 24, I give the critic the existence of God and go on to argue that even to know the existence of God is to know nothing. The attempt at virtuosity in this sweep of three paragraphs is marred by my need to refer again to "What Moves the Mind?"

Footnote 13 is very important. Some commentators argue against the view that Descartes holds that substance and essence are the same, so here I assemble crucial quotations to give an argument for this position in the case of God. I should have gone on to point out that the ontological proof for the existence of God leaves open the question of whether existence is God's substance itself or an essential attribute of God's substance. Descartes concludes that God's substance, existence, and essence are identical.

If I am countering known commentators, why do I not give references to them, state their arguments, and show exactly how they are wrong? You can do only so much in a short paper. But that is not the only reason for simply stating your position and going on. I recommend that you start out writing critical discussion notes, but after a while you should have established a position of your own. If you fill all your publications with detailed statements of other people's arguments and your detailed arguments against them, you begin to lose sight of your major thesis. More to the point, so do your readers. And you may get so involved in critical disputation that you never develop any major theses at all. You should know the literature in your field, but only a small part of it is worth explicit critical comment. I do cite the commentators I'm opposing in footnote 17.

Thus, a strong reason for proceeding by making only implicit or elliptical allusion to opposing interpretations is that you owe your readers a clear and uncluttered statement of your own position. If they keep tripping over your summaries of other people's positions and your picayune criticisms of those positions, they are going to lose both your argument and any interest in pursuing it.

Paragraph 25. This is to present the ontological proof as Descartes's supreme attempt to make it impossible in this case to drive a wedge between knowing that something exists and knowing what it is, for God is His existence. The idea of God is simple in the sense of noncomplex. But since propositions such as the *cogito* are complex, Descartes says that only what is comprehensible—or clear and distinct—in nondiscursive intuition is certain. The noncomplex thus merges with anything complex that can be comprehended in intuition as though it were simple.

Paragraph 26. To complete this picture, I suggest that Descartes further claims that the ideas of God, mind, and matter are innate in order to avoid at least those sceptical problems that would arise if they were said to be caused by perceptual and abstractive processes.

Paragraph 27. If one could trust innate ideas, then, in the order of knowledge God would be best known, for the idea of God is a simple identity of essence and existence that is open to immediate intuition. Next, mind is better known than body, because—Descartes claims—we can intuit both the existence and the essence of mind. But Descartes believes that he has an intuitive grasp only of the essence and not of the existence of matter.

Paragraph 28. Descartes's interpretation of the *cogito* as intuited is thus seen as an attempt to gain knowledge that something exists, a gambit at least as old as Augustine. The gambit does not work, but even if it did, one could not proceed metaphysically because of inability to know what the essence is of this thing that exists. The offering of innate ideas of mind, matter, and God is inadequate because their source and application are dubitable. A stronger move is to provide in one intuition knowledge both of essence and of existence, and this is done in the ontological proof of God. And here to escape problems of discursiveness and of complexity, the intuition is of a single notion, necessary existence, which is both God's essence and His existence.

Paragraph 29. I argue above that Descartes fails to grasp either his own existence or essence intuitively. And I stress that innate ideas are not as such guarantors of certain knowledge, for either the demon or God could have made them appear to refer to existents when they do not. Given these difficulties, Descartes's attempted way out of scepticism is by way of intuitive knowledge of the innate simple idea of God that presumably is not susceptible to mistake, misinterpretation, memory failure, or deception. But even were this true, the idea of sheer existence is contentless, so in the end Descartes knows nothing.

Paragraph 25 is unnecessary repetition. Why did I put it in? Probably (one does not always remember) it is because here I am about to make a very speculative point concerning why Descartes says the ideas of God, mind, and matter are innate. This is an analytic, not a historical point. Paragraphs 26, 27, and 28 wrap up the preceding points. Then in paragraph 29, I conclude once again with an "even if" construction. Even if he has intuitive knowledge of God, Descartes knows nothing.

IV

Paragraph 30. Suppose one could intuit that something exists. I present Descartes here as making the claim for this intuition in two instances, in the *cogito* for his own existence, and in the ontological proof for God's existence. Descartes himself makes the case that these two existents can be reached in the same intuition, that in intuiting his own existence he also intuits God's existence.[14] Can two separate entities be known to exist in a single intuition? Given that we are not certain that we know the true essence of mind, but we do know in the *cogito* that something exists, and given that God's essence just is His existence which we know intuitively also in the *cogito*, then perhaps the "I" being intuited is not an individual mind or soul, but—as Spinoza posits—merely a mode of an attribute of God. Not "I think" but "It thinks." But this—on Descartes's sceptical grounds—would be much less than Spinoza himself provides, for all that is known is that something exists, not what it is, not that its essence is thinking or extension or anything other than existence itself.

Footnote 14. "We must of necessity conclude from the fact alone that I exist, or that the idea of a Being supremely perfect—that is of God—is in me, that the proof of God's existence is grounded on the highest evidence. . . . For from the sole fact that God created me it is most probable that in some way he has placed his image and similitude upon me, and that I perceive this similitude (in which the idea of God is contained) by means of the same faculty by which I perceive myself—that is to say, when I reflect on myself I not only know that I am something [imperfect], incomplete and dependent on another, which incessantly aspires after something which is better and greater than myself, but I also know that He on whom I depend possesses in Himself all the great things toward which I aspire [and the ideas of which I find within myself] and that not indefinitely or potentially alone, but really, actually and infinitely; and that thus He is God." "Meditation III," Haldane and Ross, Vol. I, p. 170.

Paragraph 31. What I contend above is that because Descartes cannot argue to the conclusion that he exists, he claims that he intuits that he exists. And because he cannot argue to the conclusion that his essence is thinking, he provides the innate idea of mind. Also, Descartes cannot argue to the conclusion that God exists, so he says that he intuits that God exists. And he cannot argue to the conclusion that God's essence is existence, so he identifies the innate idea of God with the idea of necessary existence, which means that in intuiting God's existence he intuits God's essence at the same time. Finally, if intuiting that I exist is a part or the whole of intuiting that God necessarily exists, then it may be that there is only one primary intuition. I might be mistaken in thinking that I exist. Perhaps in the *cogito* I discover only that God exists.

Paragraph 32. The conclusion I take to be devastating to Cartesian metaphysics is that even if Descartes knows that he exists and/or that God exists, he can know nothing about what either of these existing things is. He cannot know his own essence, and the essence of God is mere existence. God is not characterized substantively. And thus we come again to the crux: Descartes wants to claim that knowledge that something exists is certain and metaphysically foundational. It might be allowed to be certain, but how can it be foundational? Descartes tries to provide a foundation by contending that God's essence is His existence, so that here knowledge of existence is knowledge of essence. But knowledge of mere existence is knowledge of nothing rather than knowledge of something. Descartes has no knowledge of any thing of which he knows what it is. He cannot know even that what exists is a thing.

Did you not get it when I said it before? Well, here it is again. Sigh. Of course the embroidery contains a reference to Spinoza, an *au courant* allusion to the shaky state of foundationalism these days, and another concluding statement that is a variation on my theme. I wince when I read paragraphs 30, 31, and 32. But doesn't repetition sometimes help readers think things over? Not this much. Let's hurry on.

V

Paragraph 33. Supposing that Descartes has knowledge of finite existents, what he then needs is intuitive certainty about the essences of existing mind and matter. But Descartes shows how to doubt that any thing has the essence of matter, and Malebranche goes on to doubt that we know the essence of mind.

Paragraph 34. I show above that Descartes's argument that in knowing God's essence we know that He exists because His essence = existence provides no substantive knowledge of God, because existence is not a *what*. Existence is neither characterized nor does it characterize anything. Gassendi and Kant firmly separate the what of a thing from its existence, so that we can discuss modes, attributes, properties, natures, and essences without knowing whether anything so characterized exists. The ontological proof does suggest, however, that in knowing that a thing exists, we might have a way of knowing what it is. Knowledge of an existent thing could give knowledge of essence if the existent thing is a substance and substance = essence.

Paragraph 35. Thus in an heroic attempt to avoid doubt about finite essences, Descartes equates the essences of mind and matter not with the existence *per se* of these things, but with their substances. He says that thinking just *is* the substance mind, and extension just *is* the substance matter.[15] This equation of essence and substance—like the equation of God's essence and existence—can be seen as an attempt to avoid sceptical attack as follows.

Footnote 15. "Principle LIII. *That each substance has a principal attribute, and that the attribute of the mind is thought, while that of body is extension.* But although any one attribute is sufficient to give us a knowledge of substance, there is always one principal property of substance which constitutes its nature and essence, and on which all the others depend. Thus extension in length, breadth, and depth constitutes the nature of corporeal substance; and thought constitutes the nature of thinking substance. . . . Principle LXIII. *How we may have distinct conceptions of thought and extension, inasmuch as the one constitutes the nature of mind, and the other that of body.* We may likewise consider thought and extension as constituting the natures of intelligence and corporeal substance; and then they must not be considered otherwise than as the very substances that think and are extended, i.e., as mind and body. . . . For we experience some difficulty in abstracting the notions that we have of substance from those of thought or extension, for they in truth do not differ but in thought." *The Principles of Philosophy*, Part I, Haldane and Ross, Vol. I., pp. 240, 245–246.

Paragraph 36. If the essence and substance of the mind are the same, then Descartes encounters his mind's substance in intuiting that he exists, and in grasping this existent substance he also grasps its essence. And so in the single intuition of the *cogito*, Descartes knows not only that he exists, but also what he is, a thinking thing.

Paragraph 37. Consider that if essences of things were separable or distinguishable from substances of things, then it would be possible to be mistaken about an existing thing's essence. One might be misled into speculating, for example, that matter can think. And one might possibly apprehend an essence when there is no substance there at all. Descartes would certainly want to avoid such a separation because it makes knowledge of the mind's essence dubitable to (1), (2), (3), and (4) listed above.

(Descartes finds such a separation in the Scholastics' use of unsupported substantial accidents to explain transubstantiation to be absurd.[16]) If one does not separate substance and essence—as Descartes does not—and if in intuiting the existence of a substance one also intuits its essence (if its essence is, so to speak, its existent substance), then one gets *what* with *that*, knowledge of essence at the same time as knowledge of existence. This is one explanation of why Descartes wants to say that mind just *is* thinking, and matter just *is* extension. Then if one does intuit the existence of a substance, one necessarily also at the same time intuits its essence, and then one does know something more than mere existence.

Footnote 16. Watson, Richard A. "Transubstantiation Among the Cartesians," *op. cit.*

In Cartesian studies, there is a considerable amount of discussion about Descartes's apparent equation of the essential attribute of a substance with its essence. As remarked above about footnote 13, I agree with those scholars who believe that Descartes means to say that the substance matter just *is* extension and that the substance mind just *is* thinking. Paragraphs 33, 34, and 35 thus support this position by leading to the conclusion in paragraph 36 that something important follows if Descartes does equate substance and essence: it allows him to know both his existence and his essence in the single intuition of the *cogito*. Then in paragraph 37, I again use the 1–2–3–4 argument from the model in paragraph 9 further to support the equation of substance with essence.

(I would like to think that the arguments in "Descartes Knows Nothing" begin to resonate like variations on a musical theme. But I suspect they are just getting old.)

Paragraph 38. But attempts based on essence being identical to substance fail. The case of matter shows the primary reason why. Suppose there were no existing matter. Could we still intuit the essence of matter? Yes, because there is an innate idea of matter. Thus we can have knowledge of intelligible extension even if no sensible extension or material world exists. In this case we cannot go from the essence to the existence of finite substance. The ability to think about the essences of possibly nonexistent substances makes it possible always to ask how one knows that the essence that is being intuited at the same time one intuits that something exists is the essence of just that existent thing. Descartes accepts this impasse for matter.

Paragraph 39. But Descartes claims that we can go from the intuition of the existence of finite substance to intuition of or knowledge of the essence of finite substance in the case of mind. (Presumably we could also go from the intuition of the existence of matter to knowledge of the essence of matter if we could intuit the existence of matter, which we cannot.) Descartes insists that he or "I" cannot intuit the essence of mind without a mind's existing, for intuiting is thinking which is identical with an existing mind. So in knowing the essence of mind, do I know that a mind exists? No. Because essence and existence are not identical for mind, intuiting essence is not the same as intuiting existence in the case of mind (nor is it in the case of matter).

Paragraph 40. More than that, one cannot go even from *intuiting* the essence or existence of mind (or of anything) to knowing that a mind exists. I may appear to exist when thinking or intuiting is going on, but no mind is necessary: God could make a thought of a mind even though no mind exists. Descartes never succeeds in equating—or in making intelligible his attempted equation of—essence and substance in the cases of mind and matter, no more than he does in his attempt to equate essence and existence in the case of God.

In paragraphs 38, 39, and 40, I use my established arguments again to bounce back and forth: you cannot derive essence from existence; you cannot derive existence from essence; and it does not help if essence and existence are grasped in a single intuition. Will I never stop repeating?

VI

Paragraph 41. Knowledge of existence and essence are separate, not merely because given an essence, the existence of something with that essence is merely possible, but also because given an existent, Descartes's totally free voluntarist God is not committed to that existent's being of this or that essence: it could be of any essence, or of none at all. So the arguments that Descartes cannot reason or intuit that if he is thinking, then he is a thinking thing, do not get to the depth of Cartesian nescience. It is not just that you might be wrong, but more that God is not committed to giving the essence of a thinking thing to the existing thing that thinks. And given that the essence of God Himself is only existence, He is not committed to giving any existent any essence at all beyond its sheer existence. If the way to know what something is is to know its essence, and not merely that it exists, then we cannot ever know for sure what anything is.

Paragraph 42. Descartes reaches this impasse in some part by insisting on God's infinite power to do anything. This voluntarism is the ground from which the demon rises. Thus in rejecting the possibility that independent of God there are eternal essences (for example, noncontradictory eternal truths), Descartes goes to the other extreme of positing an existing God that is independent of—even void of—all essence. Descartes's God of sheer unrestricted existence must be void of characterizing essence, otherwise He cannot be free to do or be as He wills. And of course this is a way of giving ontological underpinning to the doctrine of negative theology. God is totally unlike any attribution of essence that we could make of Him, not merely because the essences we know are finite or otherwise different from God's essence, but because God has no characterizing essence at all.

Paragraph 43. Descartes thus can know nothing of God, nor of mind, nor of matter. Neither essence nor existence of any thing can be known. This is the final breakdown of Cartesian metaphysics. It is impossible for a Cartesian even to begin.

In writing a philosophical paper, authors often hold off to the end very strong arguments that if made or accepted in the beginning would block the opportunity to make a number of subsidiary points. If you are to engage in philosophical discussion, you do have to make some assumptions, and your reader has to accept at least some of them. If I had just said outright at the beginning, "By raising the possibility of the deceiving demon, Descartes establishes absolute scepticism, so can know nothing," then there might have been room for three or four pages giving my argument, but there would have been no place in *that* paper for the elaborations in "Descartes Knows Nothing." Now, however, the paper is drawing to a close and it is time to put my cards on the table. Descartes's God may not be the deceiving demon, but this God has all the powers Descartes gives to the demon. It would be anachronistic to argue that nobody today believes that God cannot be both good and a deceiver (Malebranche, however, thought part of God's goodness consisted in his deceiving us), but I trade here on the probability that most of my readers will agree that Descartes has not established that God is not deceiving us. Descartes just does not know.

VII

Paragraph 44. It is hard to avoid some such conclusions as these. And yet, nothing so indicates the pervasive intent of philosophers to get on with the tasks of system, truth, and knowledge, as does the denial of the strength and import of Descartes's scepticism. Having read a great quantity (but far from all) of the secondary literature on Descartes, I am impressed with how protective it is of the great man, how the commentators shield him from his own method of doubt.[17] Descartes is, of course, a genius, and we all know that Western philosophy is in many ways ineradicably Cartesian. Nevertheless, Descartes literally knows nothing. Reason fails him, and he never attains certainty *about anything*. He knows it. His contemporaries know it. And his commentators know it. I show it.

Footnote 17. Among recent commentators who ignore Descartes's scepticism, say he was not serious about it, offer easy and inadequate ways out of it, and/or defend reason for Descartes in various ways are the following:

Caton, Hiram. *The Origin of Subjectivity, An Essay on Descartes*. New Haven: Yale University Press, 1973.

Curley, E. M. *Descartes Against the Skeptics*. Cambridge: Harvard University Press, 1978.

Frankfurt, Harry G. *Demons, Dreamers, and Madmen: The Defence of Reason in Descartes's Meditations*. Indianapolis: Bobbs-Merrill, 1970.

Gäbe Lüder. *Descartes's Selbstkritik, Untersuchungen zur Philosophie des Jungen Descartes*. Hamburg: Felix Meiner, 1972.

O'Neil, Brian E. *Epistemological Direct Realism in Descartes's Philosophy*. Albuquerque: University of New Mexico Press, 1974.

Rée, Jonathan. *Descartes*. New York: Pica Press, 1975.

Rodis-Lewis, Geneviève. *L'Oeuvre de Descartes* (2 volumes). Paris: J. Vrin, 1971.

Williams, Bernard. *Descartes, The Project of Pure Enquiry*. London: Harvester Press, 1978.

Wilson, Margaret Dauler. *Descartes*. London: Routledge & Kegan Paul, 1978.

Paragraph 45. In the end, why do so many of Descartes's commentators come to the defense of reason? Why, for that matter, does Descartes take scepticism so seriously? As Desmond M. Clarke shows so competently, Descartes is quite happy with probabilistic "moral" certainty in empirical science.[18] What could be so important that Descartes would be concerned also to find "absolute" certainty? A clear answer is provided by Richard H. Popkin who shows the religious origin of Descartes's *Meditations*.[19] Descartes is concerned about salvation.

Footnote 18. Clarke, Desmond M. *Descartes's Philosophy of Science.* University Park: Pennsylvania State University Press, 1982.

Footnote 19. Popkin, Richard H. *The History of Scepticism from Erasmus to Spinoza.* Berkeley: University of California Press, 1979.

Paragraph 46. Probabilism is all very well in natural science. But in saving one's soul, it is important to know which is the true religion. This is an answer to the question that puzzles many twentieth century philosophers as to why anyone would bother to search for certainty or take scepticism seriously. The theological implications of Cartesian dualism—and scepticism—are profound. Descartes's was the first modern attempt to provide a metaphysical foundation for religion. Descartes delved deeper than most philosophers have since, and thus his empty results are the more resounding. Nobody needs certainty for science. There is still some doubt about religion.

The last sentence of "Descartes Knows Nothing" is just awful. It is either smartass or simpering. Like the title, it betrays my weakness for provocative one-liners. The fact is, of course, that Descartes's whole metaphysics is based on his conviction that certainty is needed for religion. So my last sentence—besides everything else that is wrong with it—is an easily misunderstood snide joke. It does sum up the paper in a sense, but it is far too clever. Consequently, when I revised "Descartes Knows Nothing" as a chapter of a book, for "There is still some doubt about religion," I substituted the following:

But as both Pascal and Kierkegaard betray, only certainty is satisfactory for religion. Descartes's goal is certainty but his lot is doubt. This is the final breakdown of Cartesian metaphysics.

Now there is a resounding conclusion that also makes sense. It indicates that the analyses herein are pertinent to Pascal and Kierkegaard and thus are not just restricted to "Cartesian Studies." And it is a good way to end a book titled *The Breakdown of Cartesian Metaphysics*.

When I first submitted this paper, it was rejected primarily on the basis of a referee's report in which it was said that there was nothing new in the paper and that the conclusion was very widely accepted. I was quite indignant about this response because I very much approve of a comment once made by Ezra Pound: "If everyone agrees with your opinions, why bother to publish them?" I had thought—a very common failing among philosophers—that all my readers would be as aware as I was of how many recent commentators defend Descartes on reason. In response, I added footnote 17. (Anyway, as you think about publishing in philosophy, I recommend Pound's maxim to you.) Also in the report were a number of very good textual suggestions and the surmise that I could probably shorten the paper.

In the version the referee saw, I had not exactly swallowed my conclusion: I just had not put it in proper perspective. So while taking into consideration and doing some revision in response to every one of the referee's eleven detailed points (in the course of which I cut the paper by several pages), I wrote paragraphs 44, 45, and 46. Then I wrote the editor telling him what I had done in response to the referee's report and submitted the revised version. It was accepted. It is not always that easy, but if you pay careful attention to referees' reports and revise accordingly, you can often bring your paper up to a publishable level. Of course, even then you have to have something to say, and you have to say it in a way that some editor will accept.

My summation? Overall, I give "Descartes Knows Nothing" an A minus/B plus. It is a good paper, but it is very repetitive, and it lacks careful consideration of the question of knowledge of general ideas as compared with knowledge of particular things. These are difficult topics. I am sure I can do something more and better in this area, but for the time being I am thinking about it. It is hard work. (For another critique of a philosophical paper, see the before-and-after example in Mark B. Woodhouse's "Writing Philosophy.")

9

CONCLUSION

Philosophical writing as presented in this guide is much less esoteric and difficult than beginners often think. I have discussed nothing but plans, rules, and techniques, but that is because philosophical inspiration is something you will have to provide yourself. If you have some philosophical ideas to present, you could do worse than following this prudent and systematic plan for publishing them.

Suppose you publish, then what? Obviously you should send a reprint of a discussion note to the author of the article that inspired it and copies also to the major workers in that area. Not all philosophers read the journals regularly, and remarkably few philosophers buy many books. Consequently, if you want to make sure that certain philosophers see (and you hope, read) your articles, send reprints to them.

How many reprints should you get (or make, given that some journals do not provide reprints and others are so expensive that it is cheaper to make your own)? Fifty to a hundred. Besides those philosophers actually working in the area, you will have colleagues, former professors, friends you went to graduate school with, and your parents to send reprints to. It is worthwhile to send copies to the dean.

Books are a more expensive matter. They cost a lot even at the author's discount. Nevertheless, as a beginning philosopher, you cannot afford to stint on complimentary copies of your first book. You would like it to be read by the half-dozen philosophers central in the area you are working in, so send each of them a copy. They may not read it even then, but at least you have given them the opportunity. Don't go overboard with dedications; just say you would be pleased if they think it worthwhile to send you any comments. Give a copy to your department chair and one to the dean. There are others it might be worthwhile to give copies to. This exercise is going to cost hundreds of dollars? It is a professional expense.

Don't be embarrassed by the self-promotional aspect of sending out reprints. It is a traditional way of entering the professional philosophical community. Also, realistically and practically, you should send your reprints and books to key people in your area so that when you come up for tenure, they will know your work. Deans find few things more damning than letters from distinguished scholars in a candidate's field beginning, "I do not know the candidate's work."

Let me conclude with a comment on acknowledgments. Discussion notes and comments are so short that acknowledging the help of a professor or colleague is excessive. As for articles, it is appropriate for beginning philosophers to acknowledge (briefly) the help of one or two professors or colleagues. Do not list everyone you have talked to about the paper.

At the other extreme, authors of books often err in not acknowledging liberally enough. There is something so solid about a book that no amount of acknowledgment of assistance can take the book itself away from you (which means, by the way, that an apologetic comment to the effect that any errors are your own is jejune). If the book derives from your dissertation, say so briefly and thank your dissertation director. Philosophy is a small field, and what is noticed is not the book with overly zealous acknowledgments but the one in which the author fails to thank his major professor. Here is where you can recall the wonderful discussions with graduate student friends and also link your name with famous philosophers you have never met but whose books have inspired you. Thank your parents, companion, and spouse by citing their full names. And should I not also thank you for reading my book?

REFERENCES AND
RECOMMENDED READING

REFERENCES AND

RECOMMENDED READING

Becker, Howard S., and Pamela Richards. *Writing for Social Scientists: How to Start and Finish Your Thesis, Book, or Article.* Chicago: University of Chicago Press, 1986.

Blanshard, Brand. *On Philosophical Style.* Bloomington: Indiana University Press, 1967.

Chicago Manual of Style, The. 13th ed. Chicago: University of Chicago Press, 1982.

Cobbett, William. *A Grammar of the English Language.* Atlantic Highlands, N.J.: Humanities Press International, 1983.

Fowler, H. W. *A Dictionary of Modern English Usage.* 2d ed. Edited by Ernest Gowers. New York: Oxford University Press, 1965.

Hare, R. M. *The Language of Morals.* Oxford: Oxford University Press, 1952.

Hexter, J. H. "Publish or Perish: A Defense." *Public Interest,* no. 17 (Fall 1969): 60–77.

Martinich, A. P. *Philosophical Writing: An Introduction.* Englewood Cliffs, N.J.: Prentice-Hall, 1989.

Meiland, Jack W. *College Thinking: How to Get the Best Out of College.* New York: New American Library, 1981.

Michaelson, Herbert B. *How to Write and Publish Engineering Papers and Reports.* 2d. ed. Philadelphia: ISI Press, 1986.

Nowell-Smith, P. H. *Ethics.* Cambridge: Cambridge University Press, 1954.

Orwell, George. "Politics and the English Language." In *A Collection of Essays,* 162–77. Garden City, N.Y.: Doubleday, Anchor Books, 1954.

Rescher, Nicholas. "The Egocentric Predicament." *American Philosophical Quarterly* 21 (1984): 277.

Roget, Peter Mark. *Thesaurus of English Words and Phrases.* Cleveland: World, 1940.

Rosenberg, Jay. *The Practice of Philosophy: A Handbook for Beginners.* Englewood Cliffs, N.J.: Prentice-Hall, 1984.

Ross-Larson, Bruce. *Edit Yourself.* New York: Norton, 1982.

Russell, Bertrand. *The Problems of Philosophy.* Oxford and New York: Oxford University Press, 1959.

Stone, Wilfred, and J. G. Bell. *Prose Style: A Handbook for Writers.* 3d ed. New York: McGraw-Hill, 1977.

Stott, Bill. *Write to the Point.* New York: Doubleday, Anchor Books, 1984.

Strunk, William, Jr., and E. B. White. *The Elements of Style.* New York: Macmillan, 1959.

Toulmin, Stephen. *The Place of Reason in Ethics.* Cambridge: Cambridge University Press, 1950.

Watson, Richard A. "Descartes Knows Nothing." *History of Philosophy Quarterly* 1 (1984): 399–411. Rev. Richard A. Watson. *The Breakdown of Cartesian Metaphysics*, 193–203. Englewood Cliffs, N.J.: Humanities Press International, 1987.

———. *The Philosopher's Joke: Essays in Form and Content.* Buffalo: Prometheus Books, 1990. (This is the advanced course in philosophical writing.)

———. "Rules of Inference in Stephen Toulmin's *The Place of Reason in Ethics.*" *Theoria* 29 (1963): 312–15.

Weston, Anthony. *A Rulebook for Arguments.* Indianapolis: Hackett, 1987.

Woodhouse, Mark B. "Writing Philosophy." In *A Preface to Philosophy*, 88–105. Belmont, Calif.: Wadsworth, 1984.

Yudkin, Marcia, and Janice M. Moulton. *Guidebook for Publishing Philosophy.* Newark: American Philosophical Association, 1986.

Richard A. Watson is professor of philosophy at Washington University in St. Louis. He has published extensively not only in the history of philosophy, the philosophy of science, and environmental philosophy but also in anthropology, geology, and general nonfiction. He has published two novels and has a third in press. His "On the Zeedijk" is the first essay in *Pushcart Prize XV, 1990–1991: Best of the Small Presses*. His most recent books are *The Breakdown of Cartesian Metaphysics*, *The Philosopher's Diet*, and *The Philosopher's Joke*.